Crocheting the National Parks

20 PATTERNS FOR ACCESSORIES, HOME DÉCOR, PLUSHIES, AND MORE INSPIRED BY NATURAL WONDERS

Krista Ann

Quarto.com

First Published in 2025 by Quarry Books, an imprint of
The Quarto Group, 100 Cummings Center, Suite 265-D,
Beverly, MA 01915, USA.
T (978) 282-9590 F (978) 283-2742

Quarry Books titles are also available at discount for retail, wholesale, promotional, and bulk purchase. For details, contact the Special Sales Manager by email at specialsales@quarto.com or by mail at The Quarto Group, Attn: Special Sales Manager, 100 Cummings Center, Suite 265-D, Beverly, MA 01915, USA.

10 9 8 7 6 5 4 3 2 1

ISBN: 978-0-7603-9560-8

Digital edition published in 2025
eISBN: 978-0-7603-9561-5

Library of Congress Cataloging-in-Publication Data is available.

Cover Illustration: Alissandra Seelaus
Page Design and Layout: Emily Austin, The Sly Studio
Photography: Shutterstock on pages 4, 7, 8, 12, 14 (background), 23, 28, 31, 37, 40 (background), 41, 45, 48, 51, 57, 61, 62 (background), 63, 71, 77, 80 (background), 81, 86 (background), 87, 93, 95, 99, 102 (background), 103, 107, 108 (background), 109, 118 (background), 119, 124 (background), 125, and 128; Krista Ann on pages 11 and 143; Glenn Scott Photography on pages 14, 21, 22, 25, 27, 34, 35, 36, 38, 39, 40, 42, 43, 44, 46, 50, 53, 54, 56, 60, 62, 76, 78, 79, 80, 83, 85, 86, 89, 97, 100, 101, 102, 106, 108, 111, 114, 118, 122, 123, 124, and 127; Brenda K.B. Anderson on pages 90 and 140 (bottom); CPi, Chris Hubert, Rau + Barber on pages 131–139; Rachel Alford on page 140 (top); Meghan Ballmer on page 141 (top); Angel Doherty on page 141 (middle); Heather Singell on page 141 (bottom)
Crochet diagrams: KJ Hay

Printed in China

This book is dedicated to the person that I love exploring this big, beautiful world with . . . Garner: my husband, best friend, hiking buddy, and fellow adventure seeker. Thanks for always carrying the water bottle!

Contents

Introduction 6
Map of the National Parks 8
Tips for Crocheting While Traveling 10

EAST COAST ESCAPES

Acadia Sunrise Shoulder Bag 15
Congaree Leg Warmers 19
Dry Tortugas Sea Turtle Plant Holder 23
Everglades Alligator Plushie 31
Great Smoky Mountains Firefly Dish Towel 37
Indiana Dunes Sun Hat 41
Shenandoah Gone Hiking Pillow 45

WEST COAST WILDERNESS

Badlands Prairie Dog Plushie 51
Bryce Canyon Hoodoo Socks 57
Grand Canyon Wall Hanging 63
Grand Teton Paw Print Picnic Roll 71
Great Basin Stargazing Pillow 77
Katmai Grizzly Bear Cup Cozy 81
Olympic Grand Fir Fingerless Mitts 87
Petrified Forest Colors Cowl 95
Redwood Tree Rings Coaster Set 99
Rocky Mountain Mittens 103
Saguaro at Sunset Blanket 109
Yellowstone Grand Prismatic Crossbody Bag 119
Yosemite Waterfall Scarf 125

Abbreviations 130
Crochet Techniques 131
About the Contributors 140
Resources 142
Acknowledgments 142
About the Author 143
Index 144

INTRODUCTION

National parks in the United States are some of the most incredible places to visit. Currently there are sixty-three national parks spanning thirty states and two US territories. These cover approximately 52.4 million acres (21.2 million hectares) of land. That's a lot of area to explore!

Having so much land protected by the government is a vital part of maintaining a healthy ecosystem and protecting the thousands of plants, animals, and birds that call these locations home. For millions of explorers like me, who love to hike, bird-watch, enjoy a quiet picnic, stargaze, or just soak up our nation's geological history, national parks are an absolute favorite.

I am someone who finds so much joy out of watching a bear feed her cubs, a bird build a nest, prairie dogs bark at each other, or just listening to the wind in the trees; it is always beyond exciting to visit a national park that I've never been to before or to revisit one of my favorites.

As a full-time RVer, I often build our travel route to spend time in as many national parks as possible. I also look at what state parks or national monuments are nearby. My husband and I start at the Visitor Center in each park. We talk to the park rangers about what hikes to go on (we prefer shaded hikes with high probability of seeing wildlife!), what plants and animals we can hope to see, and learn the history of the land beneath our feet.

When I was asked to write this book, it was as if I had already been spending years researching what makes each park special and unique. I don't think I can admit to having a favorite park. I need to keep researching until I have explored them all!

I often bring a knit or crochet project in my hiking backpack so that I can take a break and enjoy some stitching somewhere stunning. I absolutely love finding a park bench or shady log to take a break and stitch. It is in these moments of quiet when nature truly comes alive.

As the signs around the national parks say, "Take only pictures, leave only footprints, and don't forget your yarn." Okay, maybe I'm paraphrasing a little!

The US National Parks

1. **Acadia National Park, Maine (project pg. 15)**
2. Arches National Park, Utah
3. **Badlands National Park, South Dakota (project pg. 51)**
4. Big Bend National Park, Texas
5. Biscayne National Park, Florida
6. Black Canyon of the Gunnison National Park, Colorado
7. **Bryce Canyon National Park, Utah (project pg. 57)**
8. Canyonlands National Park, Utah
9. Capitol Reef National Park, Utah
10. Carlsbad Caverns National Park, New Mexico
11. Channel Islands National Park, California
12. **Congaree National Park, South Carolina (project pg. 19)**
13. Crater Lake National Park, Oregon
14. Cuyahoga Valley National Park, Ohio
15. Death Valley National Park, California and Nevada
16. Denali National Park, Alaska
17. **Dry Tortugas National Park, Florida (project pg. 23)**
18. **Everglades National Park, Florida (project pg. 31)**
19. Gates of the Arctic National Park, Alaska
20. Gateway Arch National Park, Missouri
21. Glacier Bay National Park, Alaska
22. Glacier National Park, Montana
23. **Grand Canyon National Park, Arizona (project pg. 63)**
24. **Grand Teton National Park, Wyoming (project pg. 71)**
25. **Great Basin National Park, Nevada (project pg. 77)**
26. Great Sand Dunes National Park, Colorado
27. **Great Smoky Mountains National Park, North Carolina and Tennessee (project pg. 37)**
28. Guadalupe Mountains National Park, Texas
29. Haleakalā National Park, Hawaii
30. Hawai'i Volcanoes National Park, Hawaii
31. Hot Springs National Park, Arkansas

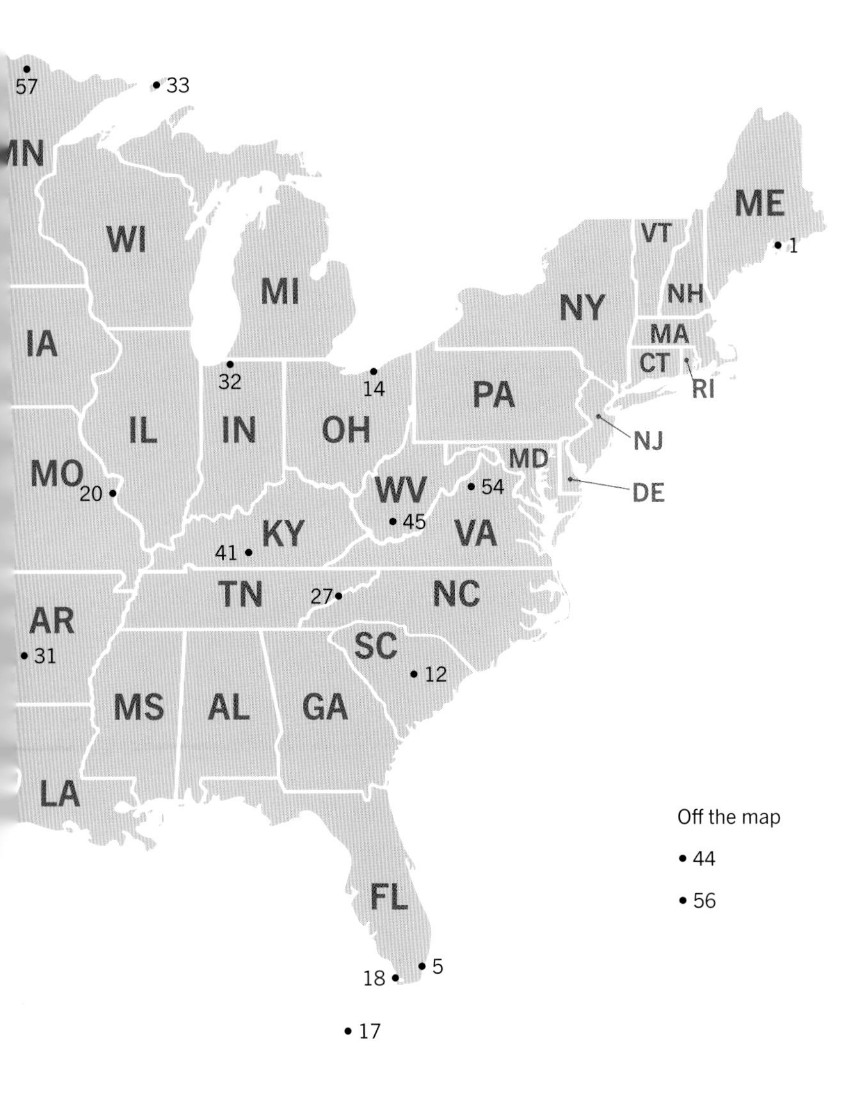

Off the map

- 44
- 56

32. Indiana Dunes National Park, Indiana (project pg. 41)
33. Isle Royale National Park, Michigan
34. Joshua Tree National Park, California
35. Katmai National Park, Alaska (project pg. 81)
36. Kenai Fjords National Park, Alaska
37. Kings Canyon National Park, California
38. Kobuk Valley National Park, Alaska
39. Lake Clark National Park, Alaska
40. Lassen Volcanic National Park, California
41. Mammoth Cave National Park, Kentucky
42. Mesa Verde National Park, Colorado
43. Mount Rainier National Park, Washington
44. National Park of American Samoa, American Samoa
45. New River Gorge National Park and Preserve, West Virginia
46. North Cascades National Park, Washington
47. Olympic National Park, Washington (project pg. 87)
48. Petrified Forest National Park, Arizona (project pg. 95)
49. Pinnacles National Park, California
50. Redwood National Park, California (project pg. 99)
51. Rocky Mountain National Park, Colorado (project pg. 103)
52. Saguaro National Park, Arizona (project pg. 109)
53. Sequoia National Park, California
54. Shenandoah National Park, Virginia (project pg. 45)
55. Theodore Roosevelt National Park, North Dakota
56. Virgin Islands National Park, Virgin Islands
57. Voyageurs National Park, Minnesota
58. White Sands National Park, New Mexico
59. Wind Cave National Park, South Dakota
60. Wrangell-St. Elias National Park, Alaska
61. Yellowstone National Park, Idaho, Montana, and Wyoming (project pg. 119)
62. Yosemite National Park, California (project pg. 125)
63. Zion National Park, Utah

Tips FOR CROCHETING WHILE TRAVELING

Maybe you will call me an obsessed stitcher, but I always have a project with me during my travels. Even if I'm in the middle of a national park. Why is having a project with you important? You never know when there will be an opportune time to get a few stitches in.

If you want to crochet while you're camping, hiking, or sightseeing, keep these things in mind as you pack your day bag.

* Keep your project small. Always bring a smaller project that will tuck away in your backpack easily and not add too much weight.
* Be sure your project is protected inside a small project bag so that crumbs from your lunch won't get on it. It also protects from the dreaded backpack-zipper-meets-beautifully-crocheted-stitches scenarios!
* Make sure the pattern you are working on doesn't require too much concentration. Your focus should be on the beauty that surrounds you—not which row of the pattern you are on! I like to work on a project that I have memorized so that I don't need to have a pattern in front of me.
* Bring appropriate yarn for the current weather. If it's warm outside, stick with lightweight fibers such as cotton and linen. And if it's cooler, enjoy working with a lovely animal fiber such as wool or alpaca.
* Always have scissors, tapestry needle, tape measure, and stitch markers within reach. You never know when they'll be needed.
* Don't let your stitching distract from the experience. Just because you brought a project doesn't mean you have to get any work done on it. It is just good to know it's there if you want to stitch.

You might be surprised just how many opportunities there are to sneak in some stitching while you're in a national park. If you come prepared following my tips, then these next suggestions will offer you a chance to crochet while creating some amazing memories.

* Always stop by the Visitor Center first. Most parks have beautifully produced short films that play on a loop. This is a wonderful place to sit back, learn a little about the park you are about to explore, and do a little crocheting. The movies can last as long as 30 minutes. That is plenty of time to get a couple rows done!
* Sign up for a guided tour. When they ask you to arrive early, you'll be ready. The wait is no big deal when you have stitching to do!
* Some parks have benches along trails so hikers can take a comfortable rest occasionally. Use these benches to sit back, grab some water, listen to the sounds around you . . . and maybe work a row or two. The longer you sit in silence, the more creatures will appear, and the birds will begin to sing.
* If you are planning to be out in the elements for a good portion of the day, chances are you are going to bring a packed lunch. It's always good to let your food settle a little before hitting the trails again. Might as well do some crocheting while you wait!

And not that you need another reason to bring your crochet project along with you, but here's one more: How gorgeous would a picture of you crocheting while standing amongst the redwoods look on social media? Doing something you love in a place you love—that picture is worth more than a thousand words!

East Coast Escapes

With a coastline spanning from Maine to Florida, the East Coast region of the United States has a diverse range of national parks. There is so much to see and do. You can watch the morning glow in Acadia National Park, which is the first national park to see the sun rise each day. Or you can hold onto your hat as you dodge alligators while gliding in an airboat on the Everglades. In early June, you can enjoy the synchronous firefly show in the Great Smoky Mountains. Each of these parks offers unique inspirations for crocheters. Grab your hook, yarn, and sense of adventure as you stitch home décor, accessories, and more!

Acadia Sunrise Shoulder Bag

Krista Ann

The first national park in the United States to see the sun rise is Acadia National Park. Located along the coastline of Bar Harbor, Maine, this national park is arguably the most spectacular place to catch a sunrise. Pack your breakfast and a sweater in your newly crocheted shoulder bag, set an early alarm, and spend the morning sitting along the rocky coastline. Enjoy breakfast while watching the sun rise above the water.

Acadia is the first national park to see the sun rise on a new day.

DIFFICULTY LEVEL
Intermediate

FINISHED SIZE

Approximately 17¾" (45 cm) wide and 18" (45.5 cm) tall from the bottom of the bag to the top of a peak (not including handle).

YARN

DK Weight (#3 Light)

Shown in: Universal Yarn Bamboo Pop (50% Cotton, 50% Bamboo; 292 yd [267 m]/3.5 oz [100 g]): #205 Brilliant Blues (MC), 2 balls; #139 Sundae (A), #118 Marmalade (B), and #113 Sunny (C), 1 ball of each.

HOOKS

Size G/6 (4.00 mm).

Adjust hook size as needed to obtain gauge.

NOTIONS

Locking stitch markers (m); scissors; tapestry needle.

GAUGE

20 stitches in Half Double Crochet = 4" (10 cm).

NOTES

Bag is made from 13 blocks that are worked in rnds, changing yarn color to create a center spiral. Outer rnds are worked around the center spiral to shape the piece into a block.

When instructed to put yarn "on hold," remove the loop of yarn from the hook and enlarge it so that it does not unravel. If you wish, you can place the loop on a stitch marker or safety pin to ensure that it does not unravel.

Blocks are arranged and sewn together following diagrams to form Bag.

continued →→

Bag INSTRUCTIONS

Blocks (Make 13 – 4 Block 1, 4 Block 2, and 5 Block 3)

Block 1 (make 4) – Use color A for C1, color B for C2, and color MC for C3.

Block 2 (make 4) – Use color B for C1, color C for C2, and color MC for C3.

Block 3 (make 5) – Use color A for C1, color C for C2, and MC for C3.

Rnd 1: With C1, make a magic ring, ch 1, (sc, hdc, 4 dc) in ring, put C1 on hold; draw up a lp of C2 in ring immediately following the last dc made, ch 1, (sc, hdc, 4 dc) in ring; put C2 on hold—12 sts.

Pull tail of magic ring tightly to close. Place a marker in the first sc of Rnd 1 to indicate the bor. Move the marker up to the first st of each rnd as each new rnd is reached.

Rnd 2: Return lp of C1 to hook, 2 dc in each of the next 6 sts (these are C2 sts from the prev rnd), put C1 on hold; return lp of C2 to hook, 2 dc in each of the next 6 sts, put C2 on hold—24 sts.

Note: The beginning of each rnd starts when you reach the m and begin working with C1 again.

Rnd 3: Return lp of C1 to hook, [2 dc in next st, dc in next st] 6 times, put C1 on hold; return lp of C2 to hook, [2 dc in next st, dc in next st] 6 times, put C1 on hold—36 sts.

Rnd 4: Return lp of C1 to hook, [2 dc in next st, dc in next 2 sts] 6 times, put C1 on hold; return lp of C2 to hook, [2 dc in next st, dc in next 2 sts] 6 times, put C2 on hold—48 sts.

Rnd 5: Return lp of C1 to hook, [2 dc in next st, dc in next 3 sts] 6 times, put C1 on hold; return lp of C2 to hook, [2 dc in next st, dc in next 3 sts] 6 times, put C2 on hold—60 sts.

Rnd 6: Return lp of C1 to hook, [2 dc in next st, dc in next 4 sts] 6 times, put C1 on hold; return lp of C2 to hook, [2 dc in next st, dc in next 4 sts] 6 times, do NOT put C2 on hold—72 sts.

Finish Spiral

Remove bor marker.

Continuing with C2, hdc in next st, sc in next st, sl st in next st. Fasten off C2.

Return lp of C1 to hook, hdc in next st, sc in next st, sl st in next st. Fasten off C1.

Weave in ends.

Outer Rnds

Join MC in last C2 sl st worked.

Rnd 7: Ch 3 (counts as dc), 2 dc in same st, 3 dc in next st, hdc in next 3 sts, sc in next 10 sts, hdc in next 3 sts, [3 dc in each of next 2 sts, hdc in next 3 sts, sc in next 10 sts, hdc in next 3 sts] 3 times; join with sl st into top of beg-ch—88 sts.

Rnd 8: Ch 3 (counts as dc), dc in next st, [3 dc in next 2 sts, dc in next 6 sts, hdc in next 8 sts, dc in next 6 sts] 3 times, 3 dc in next 2 sts, dc in next 6 sts, hdc in next 8 sts, dc in last 4 sts; join with sl st in top of beg-ch—104 sts.

Rnd 9: Ch 3 (counts as dc), dc in next 3 sts, [2 dc in next 2 sts, dc in next 24 sts] 3 times, 2 dc in next 2 sts, dc in last 20 sts; join with sl st in top of beg-ch—112 sts.

Rnd 10: Ch 2 (counts as hdc), hdc in next 4 sts, [2 hdc in next 2 sts, hdc in next 26 sts] 3 times, 2 hdc in next 2 sts, hdc in last 21 sts; join with sl st in top of beg-ch—120 sts.

Fasten off MC and weave in ends.

Make a total of 13 blocks, making 4 Block 1, 4 Block 2, and 5 Block 3 as described at the beginning of these instructions.

Block each piece to measure a 6½" × 6½" (16.5 × 16.5 cm).

Arrange blocks and sew them together, following construction diagrams.

Construction Diagrams

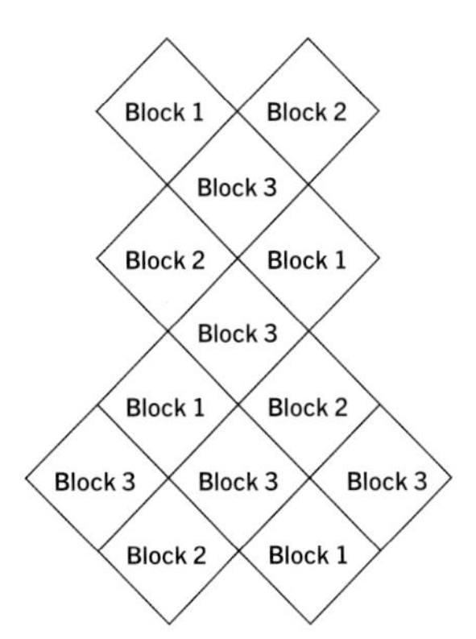

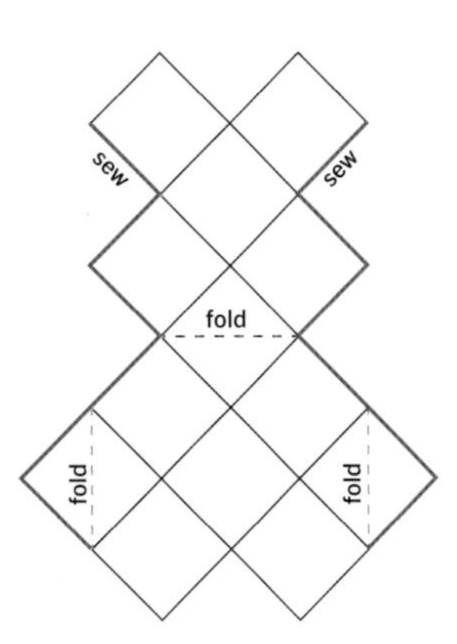

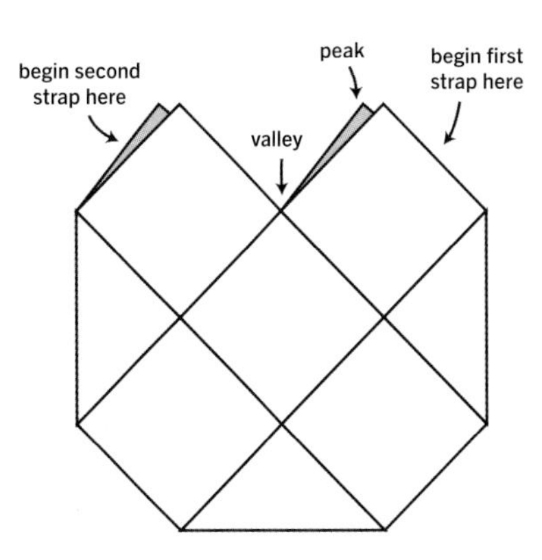

Top of Bag

Rnd 1: Draw up a lp of MC in top edge of Bag as indicated on diagram, ch 1, sc in same space and place a marker in this sc to indicate bor; sc in each st around entire top edge of Bag, working sc3tog at each valley and 2 sc at each peak; join with sl st in first sc.

Rnd 2: Ch 2, hdc in same st as joining sl st, hdc in each st around, working hdc3tog at each valley and 3 hdc at each peak; join with sl st in top of beg-ch.

First Strap

Rnd 3: Ch 2, hdc in same st as joining sl st, hdc in each st to first peak, ch 80 (for first strap), sk next 2 peaks, taking care not to twist the ch-80, sl st in next peak (this is the peak directly behind the peak where the ch 80 begins), hdc in each st to beg of this rnd, working hdc-3tog in the side valley; join with sl st in top of beg-ch.

Rnds 4–6: Ch 2, hdc in each st and ch around; join with sl st in top of beg-ch.

Fasten off and weave in ends.

Second Strap

Draw up a lp of MC in top edge of Bag as indicated on diagram, and work second strap same as first strap on other end of top edge.

Edging Between Straps

Draw up a lp of MC about halfway along the top edge of a block between the straps.

Rnd 1: Ch 2, hdc in each st and in each ch along opposite side of strap foundation chains all the way around, working hdc3tog in each valley; join with sl st in top of beg-ch.

Rnds 2 and 3: Ch 2, hdc in each st around, working hdc-3tog in each valley; join with sl st in top of beg-ch.

Fasten off and weave in any rem tails.

Block entire Bag lightly again.

Congaree Leg Warmers

Krista Ann

Located in South Carolina, Congaree National Park is one of the best-kept secrets of the National Park Service (NPS). Never over-crowded and free to enter, this park is "defined by the presence of both flood and flame" according to the NPS. The abundant animal and plant life is dependent on flood waters from two rivers as well as wildfires to allow for new plant growth. The park is home to the bald cypress tree and its expansive root system with "knees" that rise out of the water. The function of these knees is unknown, but they create a truly unique landscape. Stitch up your own tree-bark-inspired leg warmers and enjoy a hike among these ancient trees.

Cypress trees seen in Congaree National Park inspired these textured leg warmers.

DIFFICULTY LEVEL
Intermediate

FINISHED SIZE

16" (40.5 cm) tall and 12½" (32 cm) in circumference.

YARN

Fingering Weight (Super Fine #1)

Shown in: Urth Yarns 16 (100% Superwash Ultrafine Merino; 220 yd [200 m]/1.76 oz [50 g]): #BR60 (MC), 3 skeins, and #G10 (CC), 2 skeins.

HOOKS

Size C/2 (3.0 mm), Size E/4 (3.50 mm), and Size F/5 (3.75 mm).

Adjust hook size as needed to obtain gauge.

NOTIONS

Scissors; stitch marker (m); tapestry needle.

GAUGE

30 sts × 34 rows in Single Crochet Stich = 4" (10 cm) with larger hook.

NOTES

Leg warmers can be made taller by working more repeats of Rnds 1–4 in main section. You will need more yarn if you make your pieces taller.

Instructions are for one leg warmer; make two for a matched pair.

continued →→

Leg Warmer INSTRUCTIONS

Bottom Ribbing

With smallest hook and MC, ch 17.

Row 1 (RS): Hdc in 2nd ch from hook and in each ch across, turn—16 sts.

Row 2 (WS): Ch 1, inserting hook from bottom to top, hdc in 3rd lp (diagonal bar below st) of each st across, turn.

Row 3: Ch 1, hdc in each st across, turn.

Work Rows 2 and 3 for a total of 76 rows.

With RS of piece facing you, fold piece in half by bringing foundation chain up and in front of last row, matching sts and taking care to not twist piece. Working through both thicknesses, sl st across to join the two ends together.

You now have a tube with working yarn hanging from top of piece. You will now be working in the rnd. Change to largest hook.

Main Section

Place a marker on the first st worked in Setup Rnd 1 to indicate the bor. Move marker up as each rnd is worked.

Work first st of each rnd in the same st as the joining sl st of the prev rnd.

Rnd 1: With MC, ch 1, working in ends of rows, work 80 sc evenly spaced around; join with sl st in first st—80 sts.

Rnd 2: With MC, ch 1, sc in each st around; join with sl st in first st.

Rnd 3: With MC, ch 1, * sc in next 3 sts, ch 7, sk next 5 sts; rep from * around; join with sl st in first st and change to CC—30 sc and 10 ch-7 sps.

Rnd 4: With CC, ch 1, * sc in next 3 sts; working behind the ch-7, dc in next 5 skipped sts from 2 rnds below; rep from * around; join with sl st in first st—80 sts.

Rnd 5: With CC, ch 1, sc in each st around; join with sl st in first sc and change to MC.

Rnd 6: With MC, ch 3 (counts as dc), dc in next 2 sts, * ch 3, sc in next ch-7 from 3 rnds below, ch 3, sk next 5 sts, dc in next 3 sts; rep from * to last 5 sts, ch 3, sc in next ch-7 from 3 rnds below, ch 3, sk next 5 sts; join with sl st in top of beg ch-3—30 dc, 10 sc, and 20 ch-3 sps.

Rnd 7: With MC, ch 1, * sc in next 3 dc, ch 7, sk next 2 ch-3 sps; rep from * around; join with sl st in first st and change to CC—30 sc and 10 ch-7 sps.

Rnd 8: With CC, ch 1, * sc in next 3 sts; working behind the ch-7, dc in next 5 skipped sts from 3 rnds below; rep from * around; join with sl st in first st—80 sts.

Rnds 9 and 10: Rep Rnds 5 and 6.

Rnds 11–106: Rep Rnds 7–10 a total of 24 times.

Fasten off CC, leaving a tail to weave in later. Remainder of piece is worked with MC only.

Next rnd: Ch 1, * sc in next 3 sts; working behind the ch-7, dc in next 5 skipped sts from 2 rnds below; rep from * around; join with sl st in first st—80 sts.

Change to middle-size hook.

Next rnd: Ch 1, sc in each st around; join with sl st in first st.

Fasten off.

Top Ribbing

Work same as Bottom Ribbing.

Next rnd: Ch 1, working in ends of rows, work 80 sc evenly spaced around—80 sts.

Fasten off, leaving a long tail to weave in later.

Join MC along opposite edge of Top Ribbing, ch 1, working in ends of rows, work 80 sc evenly spaced around.

Fasten off MC, leaving a 36" (91.5 cm) tail used to sew pieces together.

Hold Top Ribbing and bottom end of Leg Warmer together so the RS of the ribbing and leg warmer are facing each other, ribbing piece is inside of the leg warmer, and the sts and bor of the last rnd of each piece are matching. Using a sewing needle and whip stitch, sew the edges of the leg warmer and ribbing together. Weave in tail.

To clean up the edge of the bottom of the leg warmer, join MC at very bottom of piece, ch 1 and work 80 sc around bottom of ribbing; join with sl st in first st.

Fasten off, leaving a long tail to weave in later.

Weave in all tails. Block as needed.

Dry Tortugas Sea Turtle Plant Holder

Heather Singell

The Dry Tortugas National Park is named after the "dry" nature of the islands (lacking freshwater) and the abundance of sea turtles in the area. Juan Ponce de Leon named the area "Las Tortugas" (The Turtles) in 1513. The park is significant for its biodiversity, including being a nesting area for five species of sea turtles: green, loggerhead, Kemp's ridley, hawksbill, and leatherback, all of which are endangered.

Dry Tortugas National Park is home to five species of sea turtles, including the green turtle seen here.

DIFFICULTY LEVEL
Intermediate

FINISHED SIZE

8" (20.5 cm) length and 10" (25.5 cm) width. The pot has a 4" (10 cm) circumference at the base.

YARN

Worsted Weight (#4 medium)

Shown in: Lion Brand 24/7 Cotton (100% Mercerized Cotton; 186 yd [170 m]/ 3.5 oz [100 g]): # 122D Taupe (C1), #172H Grass (C2), and #171V Bayleaf (C3), 1 ball of each.

HOOKS

Size H/8 (5.00 mm) for pot cover.
Size D/3 (3.00 mm) for head and fins.

Adjust hook size as needed to obtain gauge.

NOTIONS

Stitch marker; tapestry needle; scissors; two 15 mm safety eyes; sewing pins; fiberfill; pot with a 4" (10 cm) circumference base.

GAUGE

11 sts × 12 rnds in Single Crochet Stitch = 2" (5 cm).

NOTES

Each piece will be crocheted separately and then sewn together at the end of the project.

continued →→

Planter INSTRUCTIONS

Pot Cover

With C3 and larger hook, make a magic ring.

Rnd 1: Work 12 hdc in ring; join with a sl st in first st—12 sts.

Rnd 2: Ch 1, 2 hdc in each st around; join with sl st in first st—24 sts.

Rnd 3: Ch 1, *hdc in next st, 2 hdc in next st; rep from * around; join with sl st in first st—36 sts.

Rnd 4: Ch 1, hdc in first st, 2 hdc in next st, *hdc in next 2 sts, 2 hdc in next st; rep from * to last st, hdc in last st; join with sl st in first st—48 sts

Rnd 5: Ch 1, working in BLO, hdc in each st around; join with sl st in first st and change C2—48 sts.

Rnd 6: With C2, ch 1, (sc, 2 dc) in first st, *sk next 2 sts, (sc, 2 dc) in next st; rep from * to last 2 sts, sk last 2 sts; join with sl st in first st and change to C3—16 shells.

Rnd 7: With C3, ch 1, *sk next st, sc BLO in next 2 sts, hdc in the 2nd skipped sts 2 rnds below; rep from * around; join with sl st in first st and change to C2—48 sts.

Rep Rnds 6 and 7 until your pot cover reaches the top edge of your pot. Fasten off and weave in all ends.

Head

Note: To create the spots on the head you will be changing to C2 for some stitches.

With C1 and smaller hook, make a magic ring.

Rnd 1: Work 6 sc in ring; do not join, work in continuous rnds (spiral)—6 sts.

Place a marker in last st made to indicate end of rnd. Move marker up as each rnd is completed.

Pull on beg tail to close center of ring.

Rnd 2: Work 2 sc in each st around—12 sts.

Rnd 3: [Sc in next st, 2 sc in next st] 6 times—18 sts.

Rnd 4: [Sc in next 2 sts, 2 sc in next st] 6 times, sc in next 10 sts—24 sts.

Rnd 5: [Sc in next 3 sts, 2 sc in next st] 6 times—30 sts.

Rnd 6: Sc in each st around.

Rnd 7: Sc in next 2 sts, 2 sc in next st, [sc in next 4 sts, 2 sc in next st] 5 times, sc in last 2 sts—36 sts.

Rnd 8: [Sc in next 5 sts, 2 sc in next st] 6 times—42 sts.

Rnd 9: Sc in next 3 sts, 2 sc in next st, [sc in next 6 sts, 2 sc in next st] 5 times, sc in last 3 sts—48 sts.

Spots

Rnd 10: With C1, sc in next 10 sts, [with C2, sc in next 2 sts; with C1, sc in next 3 sts] 5 times; with C1, sc in last 13 sts.

Rnd 11: With C1, [sc in next 6 sts, sc2tog] 6 times—42 sts.

Rnd 12: With C1, sc in next 12 sts, [with C2, sc in next 2 sts; with C1, sc in next 2 sts] 4 times; with C1, sc in last 14 sts.

Rnd 13: With C1, [sc in next 5 sts, sc2tog] 6 times—36 sts.

Rnd 14: With C1, sc in next 9 sts, [with C2, sc in next 2 sts; with C1, sc in next 3 sts] 4 times; with C1, sc in last 7 sts.

Continue with C1 only.

Rnds 15 and 16: Sc in each st around.

Rnd 17: [Sc in next 4 sts, sc2tog] 6 times—30 sts.

Rnd 18: Sc in each st around.

Rnd 19: [Sc in next 3 sts, sc2tog] 6 times—24 sts.

Fasten off, leaving a long tail for sewing.

Eyelids (Make 2)

With C1 and smaller hook, ch 8, sl st in 2nd ch from hook, sc in next 2 ch, 2 hdc in next ch, sc in next 2 ch, sl st in last ch—8 sts.

Fasten off, leaving a long tail for sewing.

Front Fins (Make 2)

Note: To create the spots on the fins you will be changing to C2 for some stitches.

With C1 and smaller hook, make a magic ring.

Rnd 1: Work 6 sc in ring; do not join, work in continuous rnds (spiral)—6 sts.

Place a marker in last st made to indicate end of rnd. Move marker up as each rnd is completed.

Pull on beg tail to close center of ring.

Rnd 2: Work 2 sc in each st around—12 sts.

Rnd 3: [With C1, sc in next st, 2 sc in next st, sc in next st; with C2, 2 sc in next st] 3 times—18 sts.

Rnd 4: With C1, sc in next st, 2 sc in next st, [sc in next 2 sts, 2 sc in next st] 5 times, sc in last st—24 sts.

Rnd 5: [With C1, sc in next 3 sts; with C2, 2 sc in next st] 6 times—30 sts.

Rnd 6: With C1, sc in next 2 sts, 2 sc in next st, [sc in next 4 sts, 2 sc in next st] 5 times, sc in last 2 sts—36 sts.

Rnd 7: [With C1, sc in next 5 sts; with C2, 2 sc in next st] 6 times—42 sts.

Continue with C1 only.

Rnd 8: Sc in next 3 sts, 2 sc in next st, [sc in next 6 sts, 2 sc in next st] 5 times, sc in last 3 sts—48 sts.

Edging

Fold circle in half, matching sts along each edge. Working through both thicknesses, *sc in next st, ch 2; rep from * until only 10 sts (total) remain. Lightly stuff the fin with fiberfill.

continued →→

Front Fins (Make 2)

Rnd 1: Working around the rem 10 sts and working through only one thickness, sc in each of the last 10 sts.

Rnds 2 and 3: Sc in each st around.

Fasten off, leaving a long tail for sewing.

Back Fins (Make 2)

Note: To create the spots on the fins you will be changing to C2 for some stitches.

With C1 and smaller hook, make a magic ring.

Rnds 1–7: Work the same as Rnds 1–7 of Front Fins—42 sts.

Continue with C1 only.

Edging

Fold circle in half, matching sts along each edge. Working through both thicknesses *sc in next st, ch 2; rep from * until only 5 st pairs remain. Lightly stuff the fin with fiberfill. Working through both thicknesses, sc in last 5 sts.

Fasten off, leaving a long tail for sewing.

Tail

With C1 and smaller hook, make a magic ring.

Rnd 1: Work 4 sc in ring; do not join, work in continuous rnds (spiral)—4 sts.

Place a marker in last st made to indicate end of rnd. Move marker up as each rnd is completed.

Pull on beg tail to close center of ring.

Rnd 2: [Sc in next st, 2 sc in next st] twice—6 sts.

Rnds 3 and 4: Sc in each st around.

Fasten off, leaving a long tail for sewing.

Assembly

Step 1: Fit the pot cover onto the pot (this will help with sewing and placement).

Step 2: Place the safety eyes between Rnds 7 and 8 on the head. Position them so the eyes are lined up with the very first row of outside green spots on the head. Then stuff the head firmly.

Step 3: Sew an eyelid over each eye so that it covers the top part of the eye.

Step 4: Sew the head directly onto the pot cover. Line up the bottom edge of the head with the bottom edge of the pot. (Use the front lp left unworked from Rnd 5 of the pot cover for sewing the rest of the parts on.)

Step 5: Sew the openings left from the front fins 4 sts back on both sides of the head to the pot cover. Make sure the edging row of each fin is facing away from the head.

Step 6: Count 5 sts back from the front fins and use the last 5 sc made for the back fins and sew them onto the pot cover. Make sure the edging row of each fin is facing away from the head.

Step 7: Sew the tail directly between the two back fins.

Everglades Alligator Plushie

Heather Singell

Everglades National Park is the largest tropical wilderness in the United States and home to the American alligator. Alligators play a crucial role as top predators in this park's ecosystem. They are typically solitary creatures, especially outside of the breeding season. Crocheting your own alligator not only allows you to create a cute and unique handmade item but also provides a chance to appreciate and learn more about these fascinating creatures!

Alligators can reach up to 15 feet (4.5 m) in length when full-grown. This alligator plushie is much closer to the size of a baby at just 12 inches (30.5 cm) long.

DIFFICULTY LEVEL
Intermediate

FINISHED SIZE

12" (30 cm) long and 6" (15 cm) wide.

YARN

Worsted Weight (#4 Medium)

Shown in: Cascade Yarn 220 Superwash Hand Paints (100% Superwash Wool; 220 yd [200 m]/3.5 oz [100 g]): #1002 Mossy Rock (MC), 1 ball.

Cascade Yarn 220 Superwash (100% Superwash Wool; 220 yd [200 m]/3.5 oz [100 g]): #369 Antiqued Heather (C1) and #871 White (C2), 1 ball of each.

HOOKS

Size D/3 (3.00 mm).

Adjust hook size as needed to obtain gauge.

NOTIONS

Stitch marker; tapestry needle; scissors; two 12 mm safety eyes; sewing pins; fiberfill.

GAUGE

11 sts × 12 rnds in Single Crochet Stitch = 2" (5 cm).

NOTES

Each piece will be crocheted separately and then sewn together at the end of the project.

The main body, arms, and legs are worked in rnds. The belly and spikes are worked in rows.

continued →→

Alligator INSTRUCTIONS

Body/Head

Beginning at top of head, with MC, make a magic ring.

Rnd 1: Work 6 sc in ring; work in continuous rnds (spiral)—6 sts.

Place a marker in last sc made to indicate end of rnd. Move marker up as each rnd is completed.

Rnd 2: 2 sc in each st around—12 sts.

Rnd 3: * Sc in next st, 2 sc in next st; rep from * around—18 sts.

Rnd 4: Sc in next st, [2 sc in next st, sc in next st] 4 times, sc in last 9 sts—22 sts.

Rnd 5: Sc in each st around.

Rnd 6: Sc in next st, [sc2tog, sc in next st] 4 times, sc in last 9 sts—18 sts.

Rnds 7 and 8: Sc in each st around.

Rnd 9: Sc in next st, [2 sc in next st, sc in next 2 sts] 3 times, sc in last 8 sts—21 sts.

Rnds 10 and 11: Sc in each st around.

Rnd 12: Sc in next st, [2 sc in next st, sc in next 3 sts] 3 times, sc in last 8 sts—24 sts.

Rnds 13 and 14: Sc in each st around.

Rnd 15: Sc in next 2 sts, [2 sc in next st, sc in next 4 sts] 3 times, sc in last 7 sts—27 sts.

Rnd 16: Sc in each st around.

Rnd 17: Sc in next 3 sts, [2 sc in next st, sc in next 5 sts] 3 times, sc in last 6 sts—30 sts.

Rnd 18: Sc in each st around.

Rnd 19: Sc in next 3 sts, [sc2tog, sc in next 5 sts] 3 times, sc in last 6 sts—27 sts.

Rnd 20: Sc in next 4 sts, [sc2tog, sc in next 4 sts] 3 times, sc in last 5 sts—24 sts.

Rnd 21: Sc in next 3 sts, [sc2tog, sc in next 3 sts] 3 times, sc in last 6 sts—21 sts.

Stuff head firmly with fiberfill.

Body

Rnd 22: Sc in each st around.

Rnd 23: Sc in next 3 sts, [2 sc in next st, sc in next 2 sts] 4 times, sc in last 6 sts—25 sts.

Rnd 24: Sc in next 4 sts, [2 sc in next st, sc in next 3 sts] 4 times, sc in last 5 sts—29 sts.

Rnd 25: Sc in next 5 sts, [2 sc in next st, sc in next 4 sts] 4 times, sc in last 4 sts—33 sts.

Rnd 26: Sc in next 6 sts, [2 sc in next st, sc in next 5 sts] 4 times, sc in last 3 sts—37 sts.

Rnds 27–37: Sc in each st around.

Rnd 38: Sc in next 9 sts, [sc2tog, sc in next 5 sts] 4 times—33 sts.

Rnd 39: Sc in next 8 sts, [sc2tog, sc in next 4 sts] 4 times, sc in last st—29 sts.

Rnd 40: Sc in next 7 sts, [sc2tog, sc in next 3 sts] 4 times, sc in last 2 sts—25 sts.

Rnd 41: Sc in each st around.

Stuff body firmly with fiberfill.

Rnd 42: [Sc in next 3 sts, sc2tog] 5 times—20 sts.

Rnds 43 and 44: Sc in each st around.

Rnd 45: Sc in next 7 sts, sc2tog, sc in last 11 sts—19 sts.

Rnds 46 and 47: Sc in each st around.

Rnd 48: Sc in next 8 sts, sc2tog, sc in last 9 sts—18 sts.

Rnds 49 and 50: Sc in each st around.

Start stuffing tail and continue until end.

Rnd 51: Sc in next 9 sts, sc2tog, sc in last 7 sts—17 sts.

Rnds 52 and 53: Sc in each st around.

Rnd 54: Sc in next 10 sts, sc2tog, sc in last 5 sts—16 sts.

Rnds 55 and 56: Sc in each st around.

Rnd 57: Sc in next 7 sts, sc2tog, sc in last 7 sts—15 sts.

Rnd 58: Sc in each st around.

Rnd 59: Sc in next 7 sts, sc2tog, sc in last 6 sts—14 sts.

Rnd 60: Sc in each st around.

Rnd 61: Sc in next 7 sts, sc2tog, sc in last 5 sts—13 sts.

Rnd 62: Sc in each st around.

Rnd 63: Sc in next 7 sts, sc2tog, sc in last 4 sts—12 sts.

Rnd 64: Sc in each st around.

Rnd 65: Sc in next 7 sts, sc2tog, sc in last 3 sts—11 sts.

Rnd 66: Sc in each st around.

Rnd 67: Sc in next 7 sts, sc2tog, sc in last 2 sts—10 sts.

Rnd 68: Sc in each st around.

Rnd 69: Sc in next 7 sts, sc2tog, sc in last st—9 sts.

Rnd 70: Sc in each st around.

Rnd 71: Sc in next 7 sts, sc2tog—8 sts.

Rnd 72: Sc in each st around.

Finish stuffing with fiberfill.

Rnd 73: [Sc2tog] 4 times—4 sts.

Fasten off and weave in ends.

Belly

Beginning at snout, with C1, ch 8.

Row 1: 2 sc in 2nd ch from hook, sc in next 5 ch, 2 sc in last ch, turn—9 sts.

Rows 2 and 3: Ch 1, sc in each st across.

Row 4: Ch 1, sc2tog, sc in next 5 sts, sc2tog, turn—7 sts.

Rows 5 and 6: Ch 1, sc in each st across, turn.

Row 7: Ch 1, 2 sc in next st, sc in next 5 sts, 2 sc in next st, turn—9 sts.

Row 8: Ch 1, 2 sc in next st, sc in next 7 sts, 2 sc in next st, turn—11 sts.

Rows 9–12: Ch 1, sc in each st across, turn.

Row 13: Ch 1, 2 sc in next st, sc in next 9 sts, 2 sc in next st, turn—13 sts.

Rows 14–17: Ch 1, sc in each st across, turn.

Row 18: Ch 1, sc2tog, sc in next 9 sts, sc2tog, turn—11 sts.

Row 19: Ch 1, sc2tog, sc in next 7 sts, sc2tog, turn—9 sts.

Row 20: Ch 1, sc2tog, sc in next 5 sts, sc2tog, turn—7 sts.

Rows 21 and 22: Ch 1, sc in each st across, turn.

Row 23: Ch 1, 2 sc in next st, sc in next 5 sts, 2 sc in next st, turn—9 sts.

Row 24: Ch 1, sc in each st across, turn.

Row 25: Ch 1, 2 sc in next st, sc in next 7 sts, 2 sc in next st, turn—11 sts.

Row 26: Ch 1, sc in each st across, turn.

Row 27: Ch 1, 2 sc in next st, sc in next 9 sts, 2 sc in next st, turn—13 sts.

Row 28: Ch 1, sc in each st across, turn.

Row 29: Ch 1, 2 sc in next st, sc in next 11 sts, 2 sc in next st, turn—15 sts.

Row 30: Ch 1, sc in each st across, turn.

Row 31: Ch 1, 2 sc in next st, sc in next 13 sts, 2 sc in next st, turn—17 sts.

Rows 32–36: Ch 1, sc in each st across, turn.

Row 37: Ch 1, sc2tog, sc in next 13 sts, sc2tog, turn—15 sts.

Row 38: Ch 1, sc in each st across, turn.

Row 39: Ch 1, sc2tog, sc in next 11 sts, sc2tog, turn—13 sts.

Row 40: Ch 1, sc in each st across, turn.

Row 41: Ch 1, sc2tog, sc in next 9 sts, sc2tog, turn—11 sts.

Row 42: Ch 1, sc in each st across, turn.

Row 43: Ch 1, sc2tog, sc in next 7 sts, sc2tog, turn—9 sts.

continued →→

Row 44: Ch 1, sc in each st across, turn.

Row 45: Ch 1, sc2tog, sc in next 5 sts, sc2tog, turn—7 sts.

Row 46: Ch 1, sc in each st across, turn.

Row 47: Ch 1, sc2tog, sc in next 3 sts, sc2tog, turn—5 sts.

Rows 48–50: Ch 1, sc in each st across, turn.

Row 51: Ch 1, sc2tog, sc in next st, sc2tog, turn—3 sts.

Rows 52–64: Ch 1, sc in each st across, turn.

Row 65: Ch 1, sc3tog, turn—1 st.

Edging

Sc evenly around the entire belly piece, making 2 sc in each corner at the snout. Fasten off, leaving a very long tail for sewing.

Eyes (Make 2)

With MC, make a magic ring.

Rnd 1: Work 6 sc in ring; work in continuous rnds (spiral)—6 sts.

Place a marker in last sc made to indicate end of rnd. Move marker up as each rnd is completed.

Rnd 2: 2 sc in each st around—12 sts.

Rnds 3 and 4: Sc in each st around.

Fasten off, leaving a long tail for sewing.

Short Spikes (Make 2)

With MC, ch 28.

Row 1: Sl st in 2nd ch from hook, [ch 2, sl st in next 3 ch] 8 times, ch 2, sl st in last 2 ch—8 spikes.

Fasten off, leaving a long tail for sewing.

Long Spikes (Make 2)

With MC, ch 47 for foundation ch.

Row 1: Sl st in 2nd ch from hook, [ch 2, sl st in next 3 ch] 8 times, [ch 3, sl st in 2nd ch from hook, sc in last ch, sl st in next 3 foundation ch] 7 times—15 spikes.

Fasten off, leaving a long tail for sewing.

Left Legs (Make 2)

Beginning at foot, with MC, make a magic ring.

Rnd 1: Work 6 sc in ring; work in continuous rnds (spiral)—6 sts.

Place a marker in last sc made to indicate end of rnd. Move marker up as each rnd is completed.

Rnd 2: 2 sc in each st around—12 sts.

Rnd 3: Working in BLO only, sc in next st, [ch 2, sl st in 2nd ch from hook (claw made), sc in next st in rnd] 4 times, sc in last 7 sts—12 sts (not counting claws).

Rnd 4: Sc in each st around (skipping the claws so they stick out)—12 sts.

Rnd 5: Sc in each st around.

Rnd 6: Sc in next st, [sc2tog] twice, sc in last 7 sts—10 sts.

Rnd 7: Sc in each st around.

Rnd 8: Sc in next 4 sts, sc2tog, sc in next 3 sts, 2 sc in next st.

Rnd 9: Sc in next 3 sts, sc2tog, sc in next 3 sts, 2 sc in next st, sc in last st.

Stuff the foot and stop stuffing here.

Rnds 10–13: Sc in next 3 sts, slst2tog, sc in next 3 sts, 2 sc in next st, sc in last st—10 sts.

Fasten off, leaving a long tail for sewing.

Right Legs (Make 2)

With MC, make a magic ring.

Rnds 1–7: Work same as Rnds 1–7 of Left Leg—10 sts.

Rnds 8–10: Sc in next 4 sts, 2 sc in next st, sc in next 3 sts, sc2tog.

Stuff the foot and stop stuffing here.

Rnds 11–13: Slst2tog, sc in next 4 sts, 2 sc in next st, sc in last 3 sts—10 sts.

Fasten off, leaving a long tail for sewing.

Upper Jaw

With MC, ch 41.

Row 1: Sc in 2nd ch from hook and in each ch across—40 sts.

Fasten off, leaving a long tail for sewing.

Assembly

Step 1: Use sewing pins to secure the belly to the bottom portion of the body, then sew all the way around the belly. Weave in ends.

Step 2: Place the safety eyes between Rnds 3 and 4 of each eye. Position them so the eyes are facing out from the head. You can use sewing pins to help with placement. Sew the eyes onto the head with 1 to 2 sts showing between the eyes.

Step 3: Use sewing pins to place the short spikes, starting behind each eye and bringing the ends together. Sew the short spikes onto the back and weave in the ends.

Step 4: Use sewing pins to place the long spikes, positioning them to each side of the short spikes. Have them come together at the tip of the tail. Sew the long spikes onto the back and weave in the ends.

Step 5: Sew the opening of the front legs right behind the head and just above the belly patch. Weave in the ends.

Step 6: Sew the opening of the back legs right in front of where the tail starts and just above the belly patch. Weave in the ends.

Step 7: With the white yarn, embroider teeth onto the mouth area. Four teeth per side.

Step 8: Sew the upper jaw on just above the belly patch so it slightly overlaps the teeth. Weave in the ends.

Great Smoky Mountains Firefly Dish Towel

Rachel Alford

There are at least nineteen different species of fireflies that can be found in the Great Smoky Mountains National Park. These small beetles flash their bioluminescent bellies as part of their mating ritual. During the first week of June, there is an annual event where park visitors can view the enlightening synchronous firefly show. This incredible experience is something that only Mother Nature can produce, and it is so popular that a lottery for admission tickets has to be held. If you love these little lightning bugs, this dish towel will be an ideal addition to your kitchen.

Fireflies light up this national park by the thousands.

DIFFICULTY LEVEL
Intermediate

FINISHED SIZE

13½" (34.5 cm) wide and 25" (63.5 cm) long.

YARN

DK Weight (#3 Light)

Shown in: Knit Picks CotLin (70% Tanguis Cotton, 30% Linen; 123 yd [112 m]/1.76 oz [50 g]): #26997 Clarity (MC), 3 balls; #24837 Canary (C1), #29531 Macchiato (C2), #24134 Swan (C3), and #24468 Black (C4), 1 ball of each.

HOOKS

Size G/6 (4.0 mm) and Size F/5 (3.75 mm).

Adjust hook size as needed to obtain gauge.

NOTIONS

¾" (2 cm) button; stitch marker; scissors; thread; tapestry needle.

GAUGE

19 sts × 15 rows in Seed Stitch = 4" (10 cm).

NOTES

You will be making the dishcloth, towel holder, and firefly separately.

A beginning ch 1 does not count as a stitch.

A beginning ch 2 counts as a ch-1 space.

The firefly body and head are worked in continuous rounds (spiral). Place a stitch marker to mark beginning of round.

continued →→

Dish Towel INSTRUCTIONS

Dish Towel

With MC and larger hook, ch 68.

Row 1 (RS): Sc in 4th ch from hook (3 skipped ch count as ch-1 sp, * ch 1, sk next st, sc in next st; rep from * across, turn—33 sts and 33 ch-1 sps.

Rows 2–95: Ch 2, sc in first ch-1 sp, * ch 1, sc in next ch-1 sp; rep from * across, turn.

Row 96: Ch 2, sc in first ch-1 sp, * ch 1, sc in next ch-1 sp, rep from * across, change to C1, turn.

Edging

Row 97: With C1, ch 1, sc in first sc, ch 3, sl st in 3rd ch from hook (picot made), * sk next ch-1 sp, sc in next sc, sc in next ch-1 sp, sc in next sc, ch 3, sl st in 3rd ch from hook; rep from * to last ch-sp, sl st in last ch-sp—17 picots, 49 sc, 1 sl st.

Fasten off.

Row 98 (RS): With RS facing and working along opposite side of foundation ch, join C1 with a sl st in first ch, ch 1, sc in same ch, ch 3, sl st in 3rd ch from hook, * sk next ch, sc in next 3 ch, ch 3, sl st in 3rd ch from hook; rep from * to last ch, sl st in last ch—17 picots, 49 sc, 1 sl st.

Fasten off, weave in ends.

Towel Holder

With C1 and smaller hook, ch 24; taking care not to twist ch, sl st in first ch to form a circle.

Rnd 1: Ch 1, work 40 sc into ring; join with sl st in first sc—40 sc.

Row 2: Ch 1, sc in first 5 sts, turn, leave rem sts unworked—5 sc.

Row 3: Ch 1, sc in first st, ch 2, sk next 3 sts, sc in last st, turn—2 sc and 1 ch-2 sp.

Row 4: Ch 1, sc in first st, 3 sc in ch-2 sp, sc in last st, turn—5 sc.

Rows 5–23: Ch 1, sc in each st across, turn.

Rnd 24: Ch 1, sc in first 5 sts; working down side edge of piece, ch 1, sc in end of each row, sl st in each unworked st around ring, sc in end of each row up next side edge; join with sl st in beg ch-1—51 sc sts, 36 sl sts.

Fasten off, weave in ends.

With thread, sew button to WS between Rows 22 and 23.

Firefly Head

With C2 and smaller hook, make a magic ring.

Rnd 1: Work 8 sc into ring—8 sts.

Rnd 2: Work 2 sc into each st around—16 sts.

Fasten off, weave in ends.

Firefly Body

Make same as Firefly Head.

Firefly Abdomen

With C1 and smaller hook, ch 5.

Rnd 1: Sc in 2nd ch from hook, sc in next 2 ch, 3 sc in next ch; working along opposite side of foundation ch, sc in next 2 ch, 2 sc in last ch—10 sc.

Rnd 2: Sc in next 4 sts, 3 sc in next st, sc in next 4 sts, 3 sc 3 in next st; sl st in next st—14 sc.

Fasten off, weave in ends.

Left Wing

With C3 and smaller hook, ch 5.

Rnd 1: Sc in 2nd ch from hook, sc in next 2 ch, 3 sc in next ch; working along opposite side of foundation ch, sc in next 2 ch, 2 sc in last ch—10 sc.

Rnd 2: Sc in next 3 sts, (hdc, 2 dc, tr) in next st, (2 dc, 2 hdc) in next st, sl st in next st, (2 dc, tr) in next st, 4 tr in next st, 3 dc in next st, hdc in next st—1 sl st, 4 sc, 4 hdc, 9 dc, 6 tr.

Fasten off, weave in ends.

Right Wing

With C3 and smaller hook, ch 5.

Rnd 1: Sc in 2nd ch from hook, sc in next 2 ch, 3 sc in next ch; working along opposite side of foundation ch, sc in next 2 ch, 2 sc in last ch—10 sc.

Rnd 2: Sc in next 3 sts, hdc in next st, 3 dc in next st, 4 tr in next st, (tr, 2 dc) in next st, sl st in next st, (2 hdc, 2 dc) in next st, (tr, 2 dc, hdc) in next st—1 sl st, 3 sc, 4 hdc, 9 dc, 6 tr sts.

Fasten off, weave in ends.

Assembly

With C1, place Body on top of Firefly Abdomen and sew together.

With C1, place Head on top of Body and sew together.

With C1, place Left Wing and Right Wing behind sewn pieces and sew together.

Make the Eyes

With C3, embroider eyes on Head between sts 3 and 4 and sts 8 and 9 on Rnd 1 of Head.

Make the Antennae

With C3 and smaller hook, insert hook in 5th st of Rnd 2 on top of head, ch 4, sc in 2nd ch from hook, sl st in next 2 ch, sl st to Head. Rep by inserting hook in 9th st of Rnd 2 on Head.

With C1, place the Firefly below the buttonhole on the Holder and sew together.

Indiana Dunes Sun Hat

Krista Ann

The *Cirsium pitcheri*, sometimes called Pitcher's thistle or dune thistle, is one of the approximately 1,130 native vascular plants found in Indiana Dunes National Park. Located along the shores of Lake Michigan, this park contains a wide variety of plant and animal life. Enjoy stitching up this cute sun hat that features the crochet thistle stitch as a tribute to the unique plants found in the Indiana Dunes National Park.

Pitcher's thistle growing in the sand.

DIFFICULTY LEVEL
Intermediate

FINISHED SIZE

To fit head size 20–21" (51–53.5 cm) circumference.

YARN

Worsted Weight (Medium #4)

Shown in: Wool and the Gang Ra-Ra Raffia (100% Paper; 273 yd [250 m]/3.5 oz [100 g]): Dune Green, 1 skein.

HOOK

Size 7 (4.50 mm).

Adjust hook size as needed to obtain gauge.

NOTIONS

Locking stitch marker (m); scissors; tapestry needle.

GAUGE

18 sts in Single Crochet Stitch = 4" (10 cm).

NOTES

When working with paper yarn, be careful not to pull on your yarn any more than necessary so that the yarn doesn't break. Be careful when weaving in tails to be gentle when pulling the tapestry needle through the stitches.

continued →→

Hat INSTRUCTIONS

Make a magic ring.

Rnd 1: Ch 1 (counts as first sc), work 7 more sc into ring; join with sl st in beg ch—8 sts.

Pull gently on beg tail to close ring.

You will now be making a spiral with no chains at the bor or sl st at the end of the rnds.

Place a marker on the first st worked in Rnd 2 to indicate the bor. Move marker up as each rnd is worked.

Rnd 2: 2 sc in next 8 sts—16 sts.

Rnd 3: * 2 sc in next st, sc in next st; rep from * around—24 sts.

Rnd 4: * 2 sc in next st, sc in next 2 sts; rep from * around—32 sts.

Rnd 5: Sc in each st around.

Rnd 6: * 2 sc in next st, sc in next 3 sts; rep from * around—40 sts.

Rnd 7: * 2 sc in next st, sc in next 4 sts; rep from * around—48 sts.

Rnd 8: Sc in each st around.

Rnd 9: * 2 sc in next st, sc in next 5 sts; rep from * around—56 sts.

Rnd 10: * 2 sc in next st, sc in next 6 sts; rep from * around—64 sts.

Rnd 11: Sc in each st around.

Rnd 12: * 2 sc in next st, sc in next 7 sts; rep from * around—72 sts.

Rnd 13: * 2 sc in next st, sc in next 8 sts; rep from * around—80 sts.

Rnd 14: * 2 sc in next st, sc in next 9 sts; rep from * around—88 sts.

Rnd 15: Sc in each st around.

Rnd 16: * 2 sc in next st, sc in next 10 sts; rep from * around—96 sts.

Rnd 17: *Sc in next 47 sts, 2 sc in next st; rep from * around—98 sts.

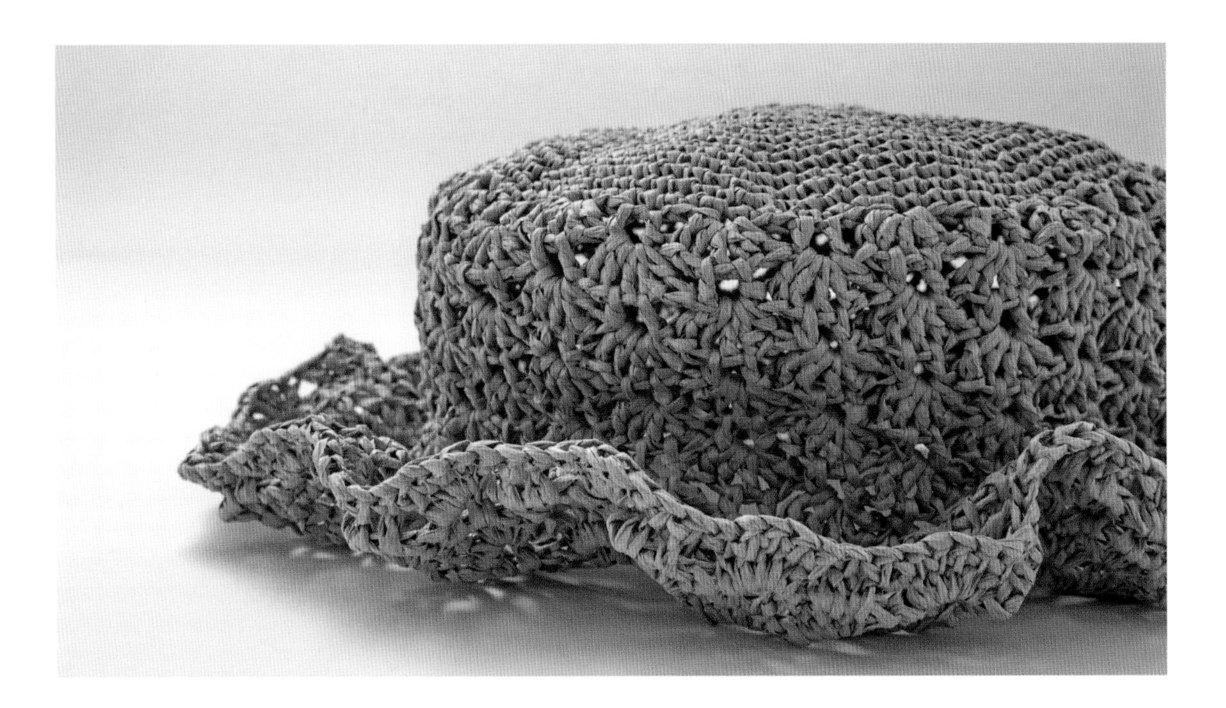

Begin working Thistle Stitch Pattern

Rnd 1: Ch 3 (counts as dc), 4 dc in same sp as joining sl st (first 5-dc cluster made), sk 2 sts, dc in next 2 sts (2-dc cluster made), sk 2 sts, * 5 dc in next st (5-dc cluster made),), sk 2 sts, dc in next 2 sts (2-dc cluster made), sk 2 sts, rep from * arounds; join with sl st in top of beg ch-3—14 5-dc clusters and 14 2-dc clusters.

Rnd 2: Sl st in each st to sp between 2nd and 3rd dc of first 5-dc cluster, ch 3, sk center dc of cluster, dc in next sp between sts, 5 dc in sp between sts of next 2-dc cluster, * dc in sp between 2nd and 3rd dc of next 5-dc cluster, sk center dc of cluster, dc in next sp between sts, 5 dc in sp between sts of next 2-dc cluster; rep from * around; join with sl st in top of beg ch.

Rnd 3: Sl st in sp between sts of next 2-dc cluster, ch 3, 4 dc in same sp, dc in sp between 2nd and 3rd dc of next 5-dc cluster, sk center dc of cluster, dc in next sp between sts, * 5 dc in sp between sts of next 2-dc cluster, dc in sp between 2nd and 3rd dc of next 5-dc cluster, sk center dc of cluster, dc in next sp between sts; rep from * around; join with sl st in top of beg ch-3.

Rnds 4–9: Rep Rnds 2 and 3 for 3 more times.

Rnd 10: Rep Rnd 2.

Rnd 11: Sl st in sp between sts of next 2-dc cluster, ch 3, 4 dc in same sp. * dc in each sp between sts of next 5-dc cluster (4 dc total—4-dc cluster made), 5 dc in sp between sts of next 2-dc cluster; rep from * to last 5-dc cluster, dc in each sp between sts of next 5-dc cluster (4-dc cluster made); join with sl st in top of beg ch-3—14 5-dc clusters and 14 4-dc clusters.

Rnd 12: Sl st in each st to sp between 2nd and 3rd dc of first 5-dc cluster, ch 3, sk center dc of cluster, dc in next sp between sts, 5 dc in sp between first 2 dc of next 4-dc cluster, sk center sp of same cluster, 5 dc in sp between last 2 dc of same cluster, * dc in sp between 2nd and 3rd dc of next 5-dc cluster, sk center dc of cluster, dc in next sp between sts, 5 dc in sp between first 2 dc of next 4-dc cluster, sk center sp of same cluster, 5 dc in sp between last 2 dc of same cluster; rep from * around; join with sl st in top of beg ch-3—28 5-dc clusters and 14 2-dc clusters.

GONE
HIKING

Shenandoah Gone Hiking Pillow

Rachel Alford

Beginning in late September, the temperatures drop and the leaves begin to change from lush green to every shade of yellow, red, and orange within Shenandoah National Park. Home to hundreds of species of diverse wildlife, this Virginia park is a refuge not only for animals but also for people looking to escape into the great outdoors! Embrace the essence of autumn's beauty with this plush crocheted pillow inspired by the vibrant colors of the Shenandoah Mountains.

Approximately 1.4 million people visit this beautiful park every year.

DIFFICULTY LEVEL
Intermediate

FINISHED SIZE

19½" (49.5 cm) wide and 11½" (29 cm) tall.

YARN

Worsted Weight (#4 Medium)

Shown in: Lion Brand Heartland (100% Acrylic; 251 yd [230 m]/5 oz [142 g]): #098U Acadia (MC), 2 balls; #153Q Black Canyon (C1), #125P Mammoth Cave (C2), #134V Gateway Arch (C3), #131N Canyonlands (C4), and #113R Redwood (C5), 1 ball of each.

HOOKS

Size G/6 (4.00 mm).

Adjust hook size as needed to obtain gauge.

NOTIONS

Scissors; tapestry needle; 12" × 20" (30.5 × 51 cm) pillow form.

GAUGE

15 sts × 18 rows in Single Crochet Stitch = 4" (10 cm).

NOTES

You will be making the pillow in two panels, seamed, from bottom up.

There is a chart to follow for the color changes. Every block of the chart represents 1 sc. Create bobbins of colors before beginning for intarsia crochet technique. Carry the main color throughout.

The ch 1 does not count as a st.

continued →→

Pillow INSTRUCTIONS

Front Panel

With MC, ch 74.

Row 1 (RS): Sc in 2nd ch from hook and in each ch across, turn—73 sts.

Rows 2–4: Ch 1, sc in each st across, turn.

Row 5: With MC, ch 1, sc in each of the first 51 sts; with C2, sc in each of the next 3 sts; with MC, sc in each of the last 19 sts, turn.

Row 6: With MC, ch 1, sc in each of the first 19 sts; with C2, sc in each of the next 3 sts; with MC, sc in each of the last 51 sts, turn.

Row 7: With MC, ch 1, sc in each of the first 32 sts; with C2, sc in each of the next 3 sts; with MC, sc in each of the next 16 sts; with C2, sc in each of the next 3 sts; with MC, sc in each of the last 19 sts, turn.

Row 8: With MC, ch 1, sc in each of the first 19 sts; with C2, sc in each of the next 3 sts; with MC, sc in each of the next 16 sts; with C2, sc in each of the next 3 sts; with MC, sc in each of the last 32 sts, turn.

Rows 9–51: Ch 1, sc in each st across AND change yarn color following next row of chart, turn.

Fasten off, weave in ends.

Back Panel

With MC, ch 74.

Row 1 (RS): Sc in 2nd ch from hook and in each ch across, turn—73 sts.

Rows 2–51: Ch 1, sc in each st across, turn.

Fasten off, weave in ends.

Assembly

Placing RS together and lining up the four corners. Beginning at a corner and working through both thicknesses, work (sc, ch 1, sc) in the corner, sc evenly spaced along 3 sides, working a (sc, ch 1, sc) at each of the next 3 corners.

Flip RS out.

Insert Pillow Form.

Whip stitch rem side closed.

Weave in ends.

CHART KEY

- = Acadia (MC)
- = Black Canyon (CC1)
- = Mammoth Cave (CC2)
- = Gateway Arch (CC3)
- = Canyonlands (CC4)
- = Redwood (CC5)

Gone Hiking Chart

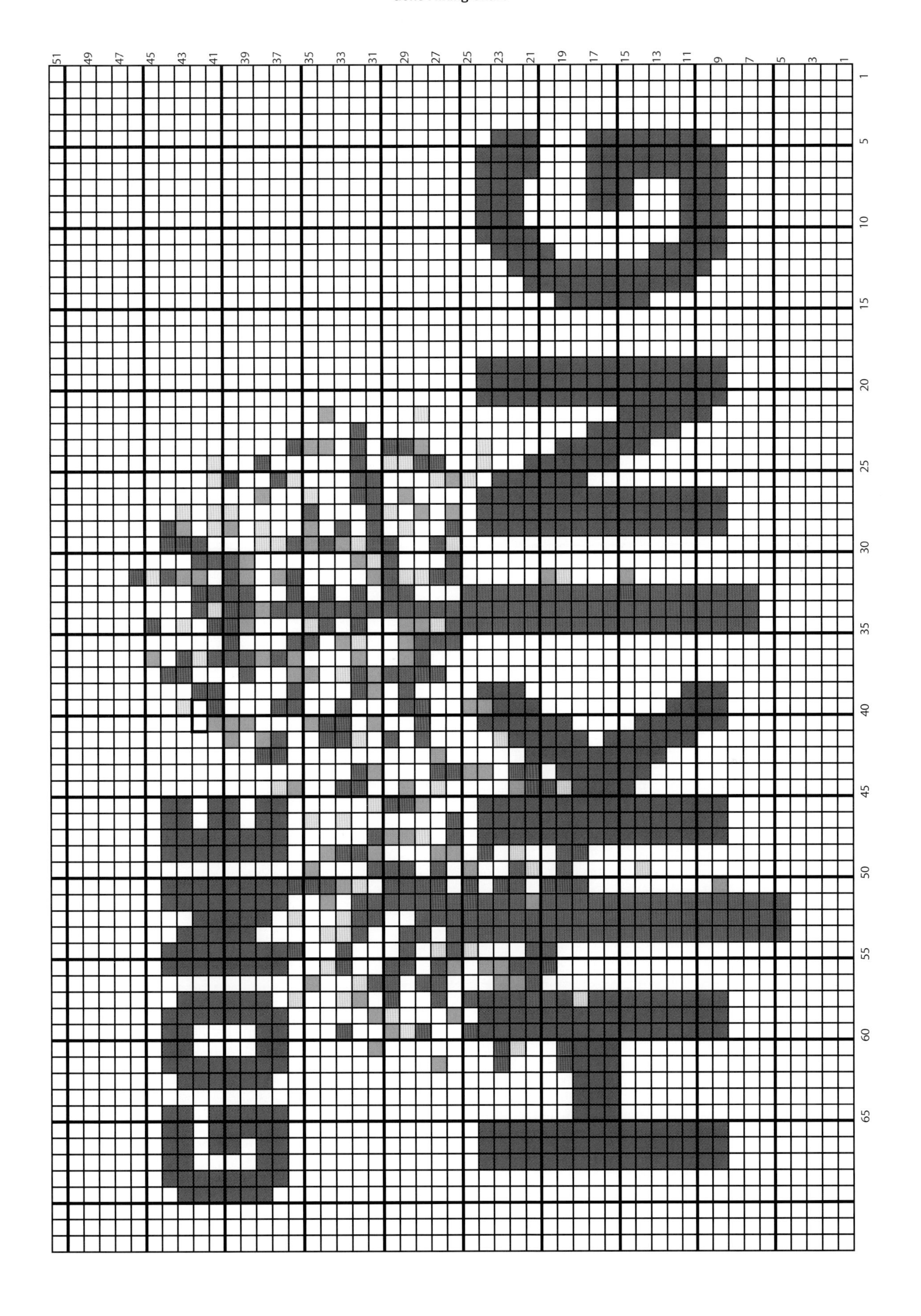

West Coast Wilderness

From hot and desolate deserts to temperate rainforests, the national parks spread throughout the West Coast are an unexpected range of landscapes ripe with inspiration. You can watch the grizzly bears in Katmai National Park and Preserve gorge themselves on salmon during the summer months. Traveling to the Southwest, while in Saguaro National Park, enjoy the scratchy chatter of a cactus wren as it builds a nest in the nook of a saguaro cactus arm. You can't help but fall in love with the sounds of Yosemite Falls as it drops 135,000 gallons (511,030 L) of water over its ledge every minute in the ever-popular Yosemite National Park. With thousands of miles of hiking trails spread across the Western United States, there are endless ways to crochet a bit of nature wherever you are.

Badlands Prairie Dog Plushie

Brenda K.B. Anderson

Badlands National Park is home to Roberts Prairie Dog Town, a large colony visible along Badlands Loop Road. Here you can see playful prairie dogs popping in and out of their underground homes, yipping and barking to each other. Now you can make your very own prairie dog for your burrow! This chubby little guy will warm your heart and remind you of the precious wildlife in our parks.

Prairie dogs become quite plump when fed by park visitors.

DIFFICULTY LEVEL
Intermediate

FINISHED SIZE

About 6" (15 cm) tall.

YARN

Worsted Weight (#4 Medium)

Shown in: Knit Picks/We Crochet Wool of the Andes Superwash (100% Superwash Wool; 110 yd [100 m]/1.75 oz [50 g]): #26319 Brass Heather (MC), 2 balls, #26317 Oyster Heather (C1), 1 ball, and a very small amount of #26304 Cobblestone Heather (C2) for tail tip, ear accent, and embroidery of features.

HOOK

Size E/4 (3.5 mm).

Adjust hook size as needed to obtain gauge.

NOTIONS

Yarn needle; stitch markers; fiberfill; two 13 mm black safety eyes; quilter's pins.

GAUGE

Work through Rnd 8 of Head directions. Circle measures 3" (7.5 cm) in diameter. Gauge isn't important for this project. Achieving a sturdy fabric that will not show stuffing between stitches when it stretches a bit is much more important.

NOTES

The Head/Body is worked in continuous rounds (spiral) from the top down.

Remember to place safety eyes before finishing Body.

Arms, Feet, and Ears are each worked separately in continuous rounds (spiral) and stitched to body.

Belly patch is worked in turned rows from the bottom up, and stitched to body.

Tail is worked in the round, from the top down, (changing color for the tip) and stitched to body.

Eyebrows, Nose, and Mouth are embroidered with yarn.

Making decreases evenly: When instructed to work a number of rounds that have decreases in them, be sure to space out your decreases. Place decreases in a different location each round (avoid placing a decrease near a decrease from previous rnd). This will ensure that you have a smooth shape and make your decreases less noticeable.

Using a modified inv-dec: If you wish your decreases to be less noticeable, try this method: Insert your hook under the front lp of the next st, and then under both lps of the following stitch, yo, and pull lp through to front of work, yo and pull through both lps.

Making increases evenly: When instructed to work a number of rounds that have increases in them, be sure to space out your increases. Place increases in a different location each round (avoid placing an increase near an increase from previous rnd). This will ensure that you have a smooth shape and make your increases less noticeable.

STITCH GUIDE

Double crochet five stitches together (dc5tog): This decrease is worked over the next 5 stitches, and decreases your stitch count by 4 stitches. Yo, insert hook into next st, yo and pull up lp, yo and pull through two lps, [yo, insert hook into following st, yo and pull up lp, yo and pull through 2 lps] 4 times, yo and pull through all six lps.

Invisible single crochet decrease (inv-dec): Insert hook in front lp only of each of next 2 sts, yarn over and draw through both sts, yarn over and draw through 2 lps on hook—1 st decreased.

continued →→

Prairie Dog INSTRUCTIONS

Head/Body

Rnd 1: With MC, make an adjustable lp, 6 sc into lp, pull on beg yarn tail to close lp, do not join but work in a spiral. Use marker to keep track of bor—6 sts.

Rnd 2: 2 sc into each st—12 sts.

Rnd 3: [Sc in next st, 2 sc in next st] 6 times—18 sts.

Rnd 4: [2 sc in next st, sc in next 2 sts] 6 times—24 sts.

Rnd 5: [Sc in next st, 2 sc in next st, sc in next 2 sts] 6 times—30 sts.

Rnd 6: Before starting Rnd 6, collect 5 stitch markers in a contrasting color from bor marker. Sc in next 3 sts, 2 sc in next st, sc in next st, [sc in next 3 sts, place a contrasting color marker in the first of the last 3 sc made, 2 sc in next st, sc in next st] 5 times—36 sts (6 sts between markers).

Rnds 7–9: Sc in each st around making 1 increase between each set of markers—54 sts (9 sts between markers) after working Rnd 9. Notes: To make an increase, work 2 sc in 1 st. Place increases in a different location each rnd; avoid placing an increase directly above an increase from the prev rnd.

Remove 5th and 6th stitch markers. There are now 3 shorter sections of equal length between the first 4 markers, and one longer one following the 4th marker. Increases will be made only into the 3 shorter sections in following rnds.

Rnd 10: Sc in each st around making 1 increase into each of the first 3 sections between markers—57 sts (10 sts in first 3 sections, 27 sts in last section).

Rnd 11: Sc in each st around.

Rnds 12 and 13: Rep Rnds 10 and 11—60 sts (11 sts in first 3 sections, 27 sts in last section).

Rnd 14: Sc in each st around making 1 increase into each of the first 3 sections between markers—63 sts (12 sts in first 3 sections, 27 sts in last section).

Rnds 15–17: Sc in each st around.

Place eyes before continuing:

The section that lies between the 4th stitch marker and the last st of the rnd is the center front of the Prairie Dog's face. Place safety eyes between Rnds 14 and 15, with 11 sts (10 holes between sts) between the posts of the safety eyes. Attach backings to secure in place.

Rnds 18–29: Rep Rnds 14–17 another 3 times—72 sts (15 sts in first 3 sections, 27 sts in last section).

Rnds 30–37: Sc in each st around.

Remove all st markers except bor marker.

Do not fasten off.

Decrease for bottom

Rnd 38: [Sc in next 10 sts, inv-dec, place marker in inv-dec just made] 5 times, sc in next 10 sts, inv-dec—66 sts (11 sts between markers).

Rnd 39: Sc in each st around.

Rnd 40: Sc in each st around making 1 inv-dec between each set of markers—60 sts (10 sts between markers).

Rnd 41: Sc in each st around.

Rnds 42–45: Rep Rnd 40—36 sts (6 sts between markers) after working Rnd 45.

Stuff head/body firmly, continuing to add stuffing as work progresses.

Rnds 46–49: Repeat Rnd 40—12 sts after working Rnd 49.

Fasten off. Using yarn needle, weave yarn tail through front lps of rem 12 sts and pull tight to close hole.

Muzzle

Rnd 1: With C1, make an adjustable lp, 6 sc into lp, pull on beg yarn tail to close lp, do not join but work in a spiral. Use a marker to keep track of bor—6 sts.

Rnd 2: 2 sc into each st—12 sts.

Rnd 3: [Sc in next st, 2 sc in next st] 6 times—18 sts.

Rnd 4: Sc in each st around.

Slip st and fasten off, leaving a long tail for sewing.

Arms (Make 2)

Rnd 1: With MC, make an adjustable lp, 6 sc into lp, pull on beg yarn tail to close lp, do not join but work in a spiral. Use a marker to keep track of bor—6 sts.

Rnd 2: 2 sc into each st—12 sts.

Rnds 3–5: Sc in each st around—12 sts.

Rnds 6–10: Sc in each st around making 1 inv-dec per rnd—7 sts in Rnd 10.

Fasten off, leaving a long tail.

Tummy Patch (contrast color patch)

With C1, ch 13.

Row 1: Starting with second ch from hook and working into the bottom of the ch, 2 sc in next ch, sc in each of next 10 ch, 2 sc in next ch, turn—14 sts.

Rows 2 and 3: Ch 1, 2 sc in next st, sc in each st across to last st, 2 sc in last st, turn—18 sc in Row 3.

Rows 4–15: Ch 1, sc in each st, turn.

Rows 16 and 17: Ch 1, sc2tog, sc in each st to last 2 sts, sc2tog, turn—14 sts in Row 17.

Row 18: Ch 1, sc2tog twice, sc in next 6 sts, sc2tog twice, turn—12 sc.

Do not fasten off.

Tummy Patch Edging

Keeping same side facing, *rotate Tummy Patch (like turning a steering wheel) in order to work along the row ends. Use a stitch marker to divide the side edge of the tummy into two equal sections. 7 sc into each of the two sections along the side-edge of Tummy Patch**. Rotate in order to work along foundation chain of Tummy Patch. 1 sc into each of the 12 sts across foundation edge of Tummy Patch, repeat from * to ** once more, sl st in first st at top edge of tummy and fasten off, leaving a long tail for sewing.

Feet (Make 2)

Rnd 1: With MC, make a magic ring, 6 sc into ring, pull on beg yarn tail to tighten ring, do not join now but work in a spiral. Use a stitch marker to keep track bor—6 sts.

Rnd 2: 2 sc into each st—12 sts.

Rnd 3: Sc in next 3 sts, [5 dc in next st, sc in next st] 3 times, sc in next 3 sts—24 sts.

Rnd 4: Sc in next 3 sts, [dc5tog, sc in next st] 3 times, sc in next 3 sts—12 sts.

Rnd 5: [Sc in next st, sc2tog] 4 times, sl st in first st and fasten off—8 sts. Stuff foot and toes with fiberfill stuffing.

Rnd 6: Pull up a lp of C1 in sl st at back of ankle, ch 1, 2 sc in each st, sl st in first sc of rnd and fasten off, leaving a long tail for sewing—16 sts.

continued →→

Ears (Make 2)

Row 1: With MC, make a magic ring, 6 sc into ring, pull on beg yarn tail to tighten ring, turn—6 sts.

Row 2: Ch 1, sc in each st, turn.

Row 3: Ch 1, sl st in each st.

Fasten off, leaving a long tail for sewing.

Tail

Rnd 1: With C2, make a magic ring, 8 sc into ring, pull on beg yarn tail to close ring, do not join now but work in a spiral—8 sts.

Rnds 2–5: Sc in each st around.

Sl st and fasten off.

Rnd 6: Leaving long tail, make slip knot with MC and place on hook. With slip knot of MC on hook, and starting with any st from last rnd of C2, sc in each st, do not join but work in a spiral. Leave beg yarn tail hanging on outside of tail as it is created. This will be used later for embroidered detail.

Rnd 7: Sc in next 4 sts, 2 sc in next st, sc in next 3 sts—9 sts.

Rnds 8–14: Sc in each st.

Fasten off, leaving a long tail for sewing. Stuff tail lightly with fiberfill.

Use MC beg yarn tail to embroider 8 to 9 vertical lines of MC that extend into the C2 section.

Finishing

Block any pieces if necessary. Stuff Muzzle with fiberfill, then pin Muzzle to face using photos for reference. The top of the Muzzle should align with the rnd between eyes. Use yarn tails to whip stitch edges of Muzzle in place. Pin Tummy Patch to front of Body, whip stitch in place around all edges. Stuff each foot with fiberfill, then pin each foot to front of Body, just within lower corners of Tummy Patch. With C1 yarn tails, stitch each foot to Body. Stuff each arm with a small amount of fiberfill. Flatten arm opening, pin to Body just to the outside of Tummy Patch and whip stitch arms in place. Stuff Tail lightly, then sew Tail to back of Prairie Dog using yarn tails and yarn needle. Using yarn needle and C2, embroider a triangle for a nose, make a short vertical stitch beneath nose, and make an upside down V for mouth. With C2, make a short, dashed line above each eye for eyebrows using photos for reference. Weave in ends.

Bryce Canyon Hoodoo Socks

Brenda K. B. Anderson

Bryce Canyon is home to the largest collection of hoodoos in the world. Due to the high amount of iron in the rock, these unique, tall spindles of rock are a gorgeous red color, and they contrast beautifully with the clear bright blue sky beyond their peaks. With just four simple rounds of colorwork, you can paint a picture of the beautiful rocky terrain of Bryce Canyon onto the cuff of these comfortable hiking socks.

"Hoodoos" are the unique rock shapes seen in Bryce Canyon National Park.

DIFFICULTY LEVEL
Intermediate

FINISHED SIZES

Adult S (M, L)

Finished circumference: 7" (7¾", 8½") [18 (19.5, 21.5) cm] around foot/ankle.

Finished length: 8" (9", 10") [20.5 (23, 25.5) cm], from toe to heel corner, excluding gusset.

Notes: These socks fit best when socks measure between 0" to ½" (0 to 1.5 cm) smaller than actual foot/ankle circumference (your body measurement) and about 1" (2.5 cm) shorter than foot measurement. Socks will comfortably stretch about 1" to 2" (2.5 to 5 cm) in width. Choose size based on foot circumference. Notes are given within the pattern for adjusting foot and ankle length. Adjusting length/size may change yarn amounts. Sample shown is size M.

YARN

Fingering Weight (#1 Super Fine)

Shown in: Dream in Color Smooshy (85% Superwash Merino; 15% Nylon, 420 yd [384 m]/4 oz [114 g]): #738 Chili (MC) and #756 Way Cool (CC), 1 hank of each.

HOOKS

Size C/2 (2.75 mm).

Adjust hook size as needed to obtain gauge.

NOTIONS

Removeable stitch markers, tapestry needle.

GAUGE

26 sts × 18 rnds in Extended Single Crochet (esc) = 4" (10 cm), blocked.

NOTES

Sock is worked toe-up in continuous rounds (spiral).

Use a stitch marker to keep track of beginning of rounds.

Increases and decreases shape the heel gusset. Stitches are skipped for heel to be worked later.

Heel is worked after ankle is finished.

continued →→

COLORWORK

Ankle is worked in the round, changing between post stitches worked with MC and esc stitches worked with CC, to create texture and the appearance of the hoodoos against the sky.

There are 3 charts included, one for each size given in pattern. Be sure to work from the chart with the correct number of stitches.

Read charts from bottom to top and right to left. Work each line of the chart twice before moving up to the next line (on the next rnd). If you are a left-handed crocheter, make a mirror image copy of the chart, then work the chart from left to right.

Work all MC sts in colorwork section with FPdc. When working FPdc stitches, carry the CC loosely across the WS of work when not in use. This will create floats across the WS of your work. When there are more than 2 FPdc sts in a row, be sure to catch these floats by twisting the MC around the CC as follows:

Floats should be caught every other stitch so that floats remain short. To catch a float, twist yarns around each other after the first "yo pull through 2 lps" of the FPdc stitch. In other words: Yo, insert hook from front to back to front around the post of indicated st, yo and pull up lp, yo and pull through 2 lps, twist yarns around each other (1 full revolution), yo and pull through 2 lps. Make sure that these floats are loose enough so that the fabric still has enough stretch to get over your heel. This is especially important on the first round of colorwork. If the floats constrict work too much, the CC yarn can be cut at the halfway point between CC stitches and woven into the CC sts (weave these yarn tails in vertically to allow more stretch).

Work all CC sts in colorwork section with esc. When working the esc sts with the CC, carry the MC (that is not in use) across the top edge of work, crocheting over the MC strand (or encasing the floats) as you stitch. Make sure the floats are not too tight, or they will constrict your work and will not allow the ankle to have enough stretch.

STITCH GUIDE

Extended Single Crochet (esc): Insert hook in next st, yo and pull up lp, yo and pull through 1 lp, yo and pull through 2 lps.

Extended Single Crochet decrease (esc2tog): Insert hook under *front* lp of next st, insert hook under *both lps* (as normal) of following st, yo and pull up lp (through both sts), yo and pull through 1 lp, yo and pull through 2 lps—1 st decreased.

Front post double crochet (FPdc): Yo, insert hook from front to back to front around the post of indicated st, yo and pull up lp, (yo and pull through 2 lps) twice.

Front post treble crochet (FPtr): Yo twice, insert hook from front to back to front around the post of indicated st, yo and pull up lp, (yo and pull through 2 lps) 3 times.

Size Small Chart

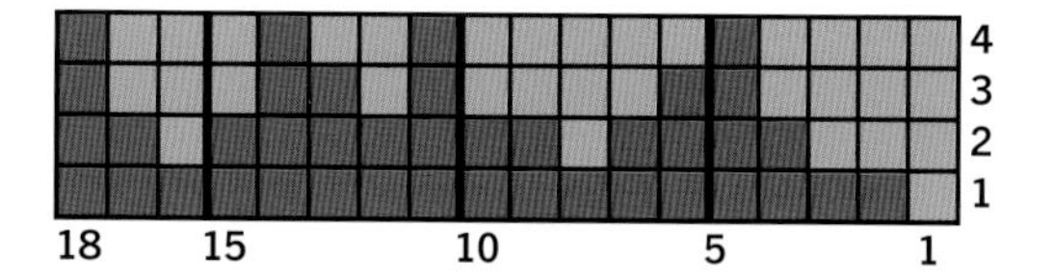

Size Medium Chart

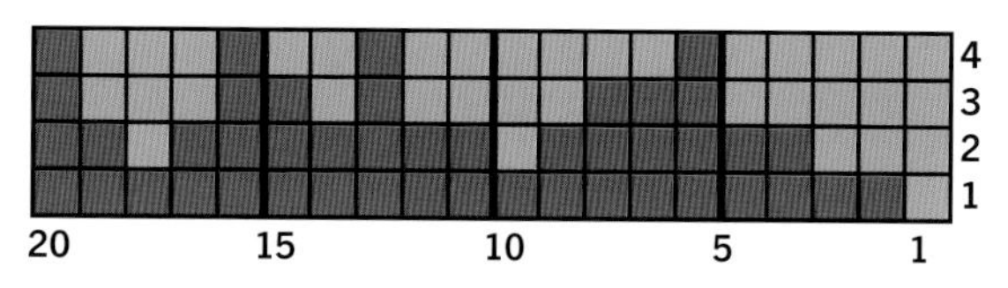

Size Large Chart

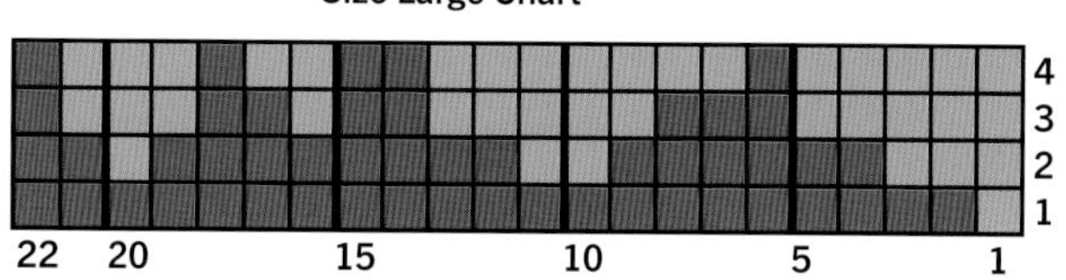

CHART KEY

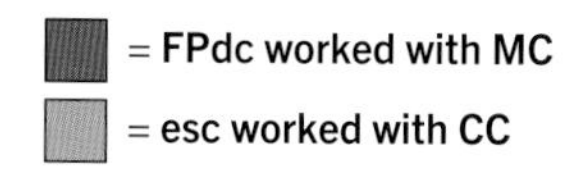

Sock INSTRUCTIONS

From the Toe Up

With MC, ch 9.

Set-up Row: Working into back bumps of foundation ch, sc in 2nd ch from hook and in each ch across, do NOT turn—8 sc.

Rnd 1: Rotate piece 180 degrees (like turning a steering wheel) to work along opposite side of foundation ch, 2 esc in each of next 2 sts, esc in next 4 sts, 2 esc in each of next 2 sts; rotate piece 180 degrees, sk turning ch, 2 esc in each of next 2 sts, esc next 4 sts, 2 esc in each of next 2 sts; do not join, work in continuous rnds (spiral)—24 esc.

Place a marker in the first st to indicate the bor. Move marker up as each rnd is worked.

Rnd 2: 2 esc in next st, esc in next 10 sts, 2 esc in next st, place a marker in last esc made to indicate a location where shaping (increases and decreases) will be worked, 2 esc in next st, esc in next 10 sts, 2 esc in last st—28 sts.

Next 1 (2, 3) rnds: 2 esc in next st, esc in each st to shaping marker, 2 esc in marked st and move marker to last esc made, 2 esc in next st, esc in each st to last st, 2 esc in last st—32 (36, 40) sts in last rnd worked.

Continue to move shaping marker up as each rnd is worked.

Next rnd: Esc in each st around.

Next rnd: 2 esc in next st, esc in each st to shaping marker, 2 esc in marked st, 2 esc in next st, esc in each st to last st, 2 esc in last st—36 (40, 44) sts.

Rep last rnd until piece measures 5" (5½", 6½") [2.5 (3, 3.5) cm] from beg.

Do not fasten off.

Work more or fewer rnds here to lengthen or shorten foot. Gusset and heel will add approximately 3" (3¼", 3½") [7.5 (8.5, 9) cm] to foot length. Two rnds worked changes foot length by just shy of ½" (1.25 cm).

Shape Gusset

Rnd 1 (inc rnd): 2 esc in next st, esc in each st to shaping marker, 2 esc in marked st, 2 esc in next st, esc in each st to last st, 2 esc in last st—40 (44, 48) sts.

Rnd 2: Esc in each st around.

Rnds 3–6: Rep Rnds 1 and 2 twice—48 (52, 56) sts in Rnd 6.

Rnd 7 (create heel opening): Esc in next 2 sts, ch 20 (22, 24) for heel opening, sk next 20 (22, 24) sts, esc in next 26 (28, 30) sts. Place a marker in the post of the esc *before* the heel ch and in the first esc *after* the heel ch. You will refer to these markers later when working the heel. Leave heel markers in place, do not move heel markers up as each rnd is worked. Continue to move the shaping marker up as each rnd is worked.

Rnd 8: Esc in each st and ch around.

Rnd 9: Esc2tog, esc in each st to 1 st before shaping marker, esc2tog and move marker to esc2tog just made, esc2tog, esc in each st to last 2 sts, esc2tog—44 (48, 52) sts.

Rnds 10–13: Rep Rnds 8 and 9 twice more; remove shaping marker while working last rnd—36 (40, 44) esc.

Rnds 14–16: Esc in each st around; Work more or fewer rnds here to change the length of the ankle.

Do not fasten off.

Cuff

Rnds 1–3: FPdc in each st around; change to CC in last st.

Rnds 4–7: Work next 4 rnds following the chart for your size (the chart that has one-half the number of sts as your sock). Begin at bottom right corner of chart (bottom left, if you crochet left-handed) and read each row from right to left. Each square of chart represents 1 st. If the square is MC-colored work an FPdc with MC. If the square is CC-colored, work an esc with CC. Work each row of the chart twice per rnd.

Cut MC, and continue with CC.

continued →→

Rnds 8–10: Esc in each st around.

Rnd 11: Sl st in next st, reverse single crochet in each st around.

Fasten off.

Heel

Rnd 1: Hold sock with toe pointing down toward your lap, and heel opening ready to work into. Locate the marked stitch on the right side of the opening (left side for left-handed crocheters) and note that the post is comprised of two V shapes, one stacked on top of the other. Insert hook into the bottom V of this marked post and pull up a lp, ch 1, esc in same sp, esc in next 20 (22, 24) skipped heel sts, esc in each of the two Vs that comprise the next marked post at corner of heel, rotate sock in order to work 1 esc in the bottom of next 20 (22, 24) ch, esc in the top V from the first marked post. Do not join but work in continuous rnds—44 (48, 52) sts.

Remove the heel markers.

Rnd 2: Esc2tog, esc in next 18 (20, 22) sts, esc2tog, place a marker in esc2tog just made to indicate shaping location, esc2tog, esc in each st to last 2 sts, esc2tog—40 (44, 48) sts.

Rnds 3–6 (7, 8): Esc2tog, esc in each st to 1 st before shaping marker, [esc2tog] twice, esc in each st to last 2 sts, esc2tog; remove shaping marker while working last rnd—24 (24, 24) sts.

Rnd 7 (8, 9): [Esc2tog twice, esc in next 4 sts, esc2tog twice] twice—16 sts.

Fasten off, leaving a long tail for sewing.

Finishing

Sew seam in heel with whip stitch. Use yarn tails to close up any small holes at corner of heel, then weave in all ends. Block.

Grand Canyon Wall Hanging

Krista Ann

Carved by the Colorado River, the Grand Canyon is breathtakingly impressive and can even be seen from space! Snaking along the Southwestern landscape, the Grand Canyon is 277 miles (446 km) long, up to 18 miles (29 km) wide, and a mile (1.5 km) deep at its deepest. Due to the rich iron oxide in the rocks that make up this canyon, the distinctive red coloring of the natural landscape makes it a popular destination for anyone who loves a spectacular view and a peaceful place to sit and stitch.

Cacti can be found around the rim of the Grand Canyon.

DIFFICULTY LEVEL
Intermediate

FINISHED SIZE

19" (48.5 cm) wide and 21" (53.5 cm) tall, not including wooden dowel and hanging string.

YARN

Worsted Weight (#4, Medium)

Shown in: Berroco Vintage (52% Acrylic, 40% Wool, 8% Nylon); 218 yd [199 m]/3.5 oz [100 g]): #5144 Cork (C1), #5170 Sapphire (C2), #5173 Red Pepper (C3), #5174 Rye (C4), #5162 Envy (C5), #5175 Fennel (C6), #5189 Charcoal (C7), and #5101 Mochi (C8), 1 skein of each.

HOOK

Size H/8 (5.0 mm).

Adjust hook size as needed to obtain gauge.

NOTIONS

Scissors; 21" (53.5 cm) long ½" (13 mm) diameter wooden dowel; tapestry needle.

GAUGE

21 sts × 25 rows in Single Crochet Stitch = 4" (10 cm).

NOTES

This wall hanging is crocheted following two charts. The first chart shows the background color pattern. The second chart shows the details cross stitched on top of the background.

continued →→

Wall Hanging INSTRUCTIONS

With C1, ch 89.

Rows 1–45: With C1, sc in 2nd ch from hook and in each ch across, turn—88 sc.

Rows 2–44: With C1, ch 1, sc in each st across.

Row 45: Ch 1, sc in each st across AND change yarn color following Row 46 of background chart.

Rows 46–103: Ch 1, sc in each st across AND change yarn color following next row of background chart.

Rows 104–120: With C2, ch 1, sc in each st across.

Fasten off.

Weave in all ends. Block piece and let dry.

Cross Stitch

Embroider details on top of background, following cross stitch chart.

Weave in any rem ends.

Border

Rnd 1 (RS): From RS, join C7 with sl st anywhere along outer edge of piece, ch 1, hdc evenly spaced all the way around outer edge, working 3 hdc in each corner; join with sl st in beg ch-1.

Rnds 2 and 3: Ch 1, hdc in each st around, working 3 hdc in center hdc of each 3-hdc corner; join with sl st in beg ch-1.

Fasten off.

Weave in all rem tails. Block piece again as needed.

Adding Dowel

Hold dowel parallel with top of piece. Join C7 with sl st in top right corner. Hold working yarn in front, insert hook from front to back in same st, bring working yarn over top of dowel to back, yo and draw through st and lp on hook; * insert hook around post of next st, bring working yarn over top of dowel to front, yo and draw through st and lp on hook; insert hook from front to back in next st along top of piece. Bring working yarn over top of dowel to back, yo and draw lp through st and lp on hook; rep from * until you have worked all sts along top of piece.

Do not fasten off.

To finish, crochet a chain about 21" (53.5 cm) long. Fasten off, leaving a long tail. Wrap tail around beg end of dowel and tie a knot. Weave in ends.

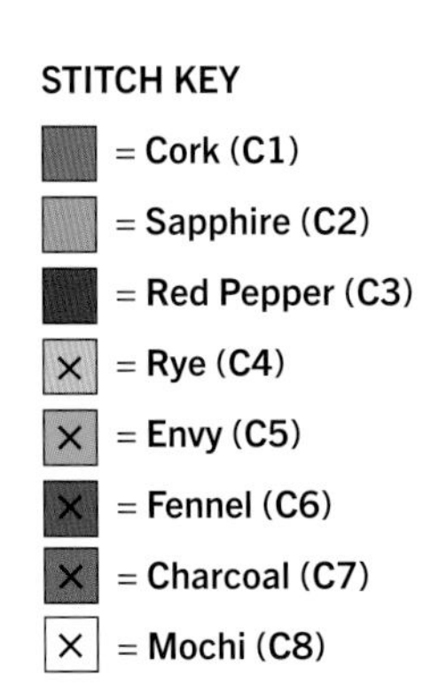

continued →→

Background Colorwork Chart

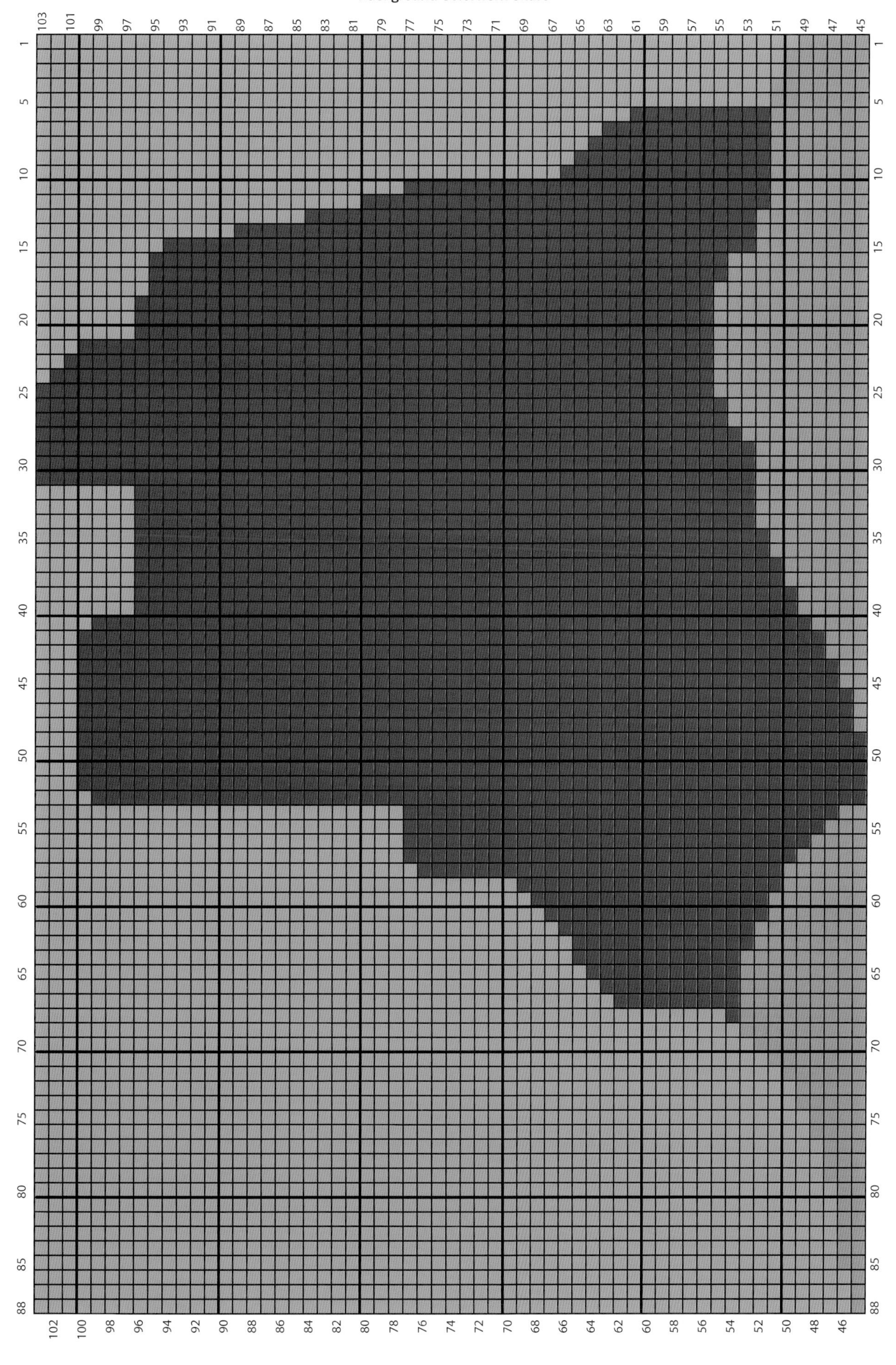

Lower Left Cross Stitch Chart

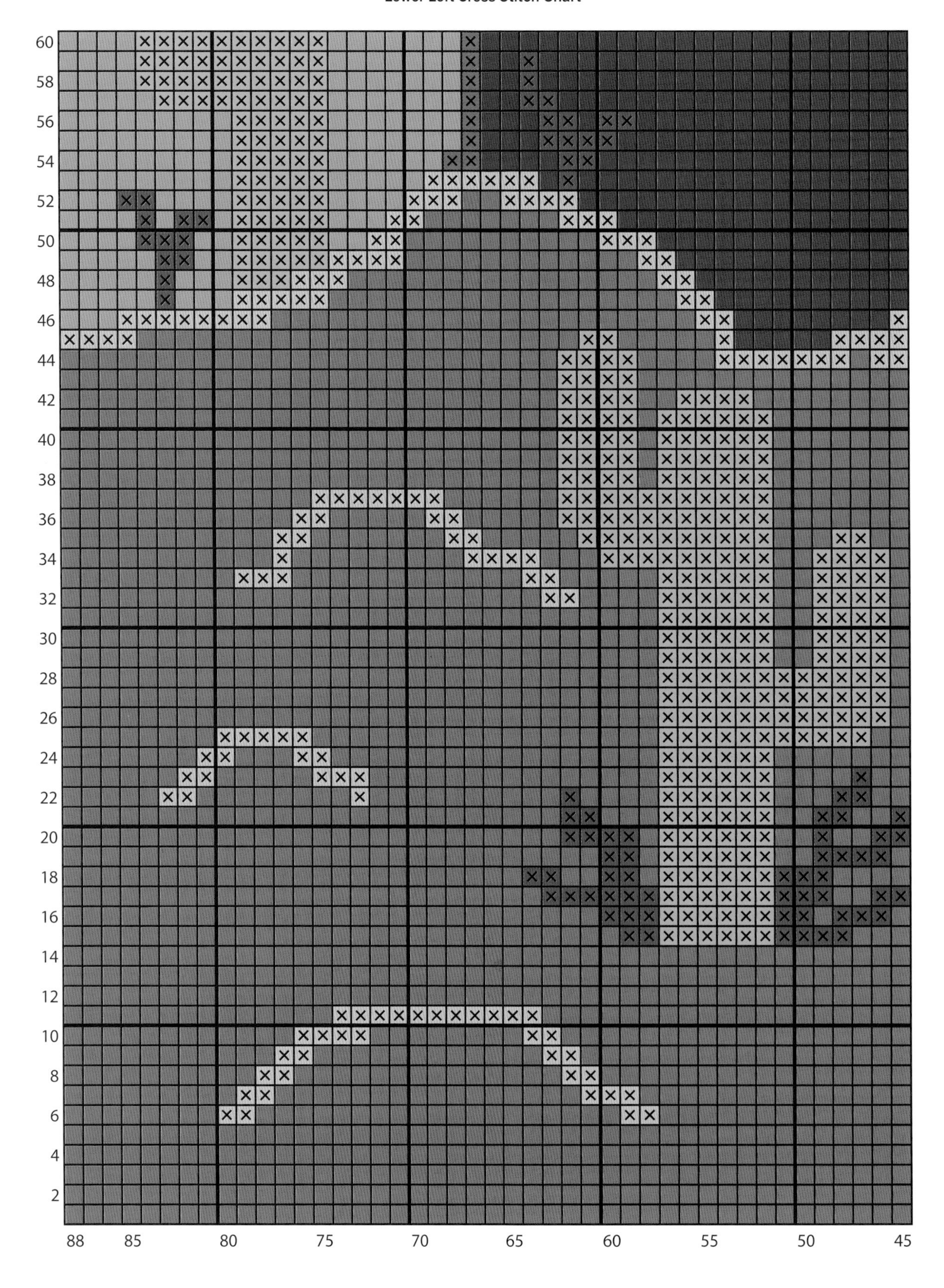

Lower Right Cross Stitch Chart

59
57
55
53
51
49
47
45
43
41
39
37
35
33
31
29
27
25
23
21
19
17
15
13
11
9
7
5
3
1

40 35 30 25 20 15 10 5 1

Upper Left Cross Stitch Chart

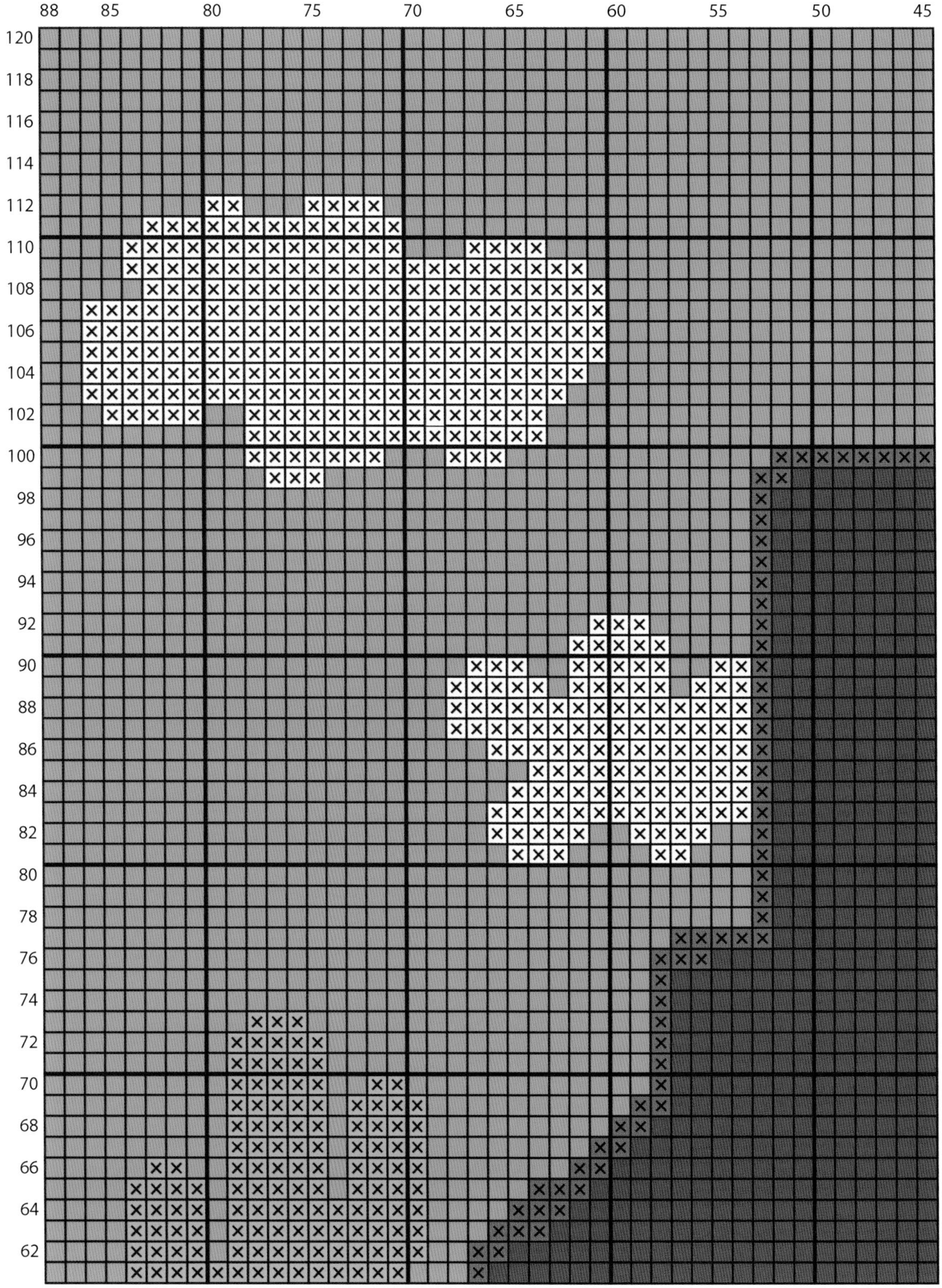

88 85 80 75 70 65 60 55 50 45

120 118 116 114 112 110 108 106 104 102 100 98 96 94 92 90 88 86 84 82 80 78 76 74 72 70 68 66 64 62

Upper Right Cross Stitch Chart

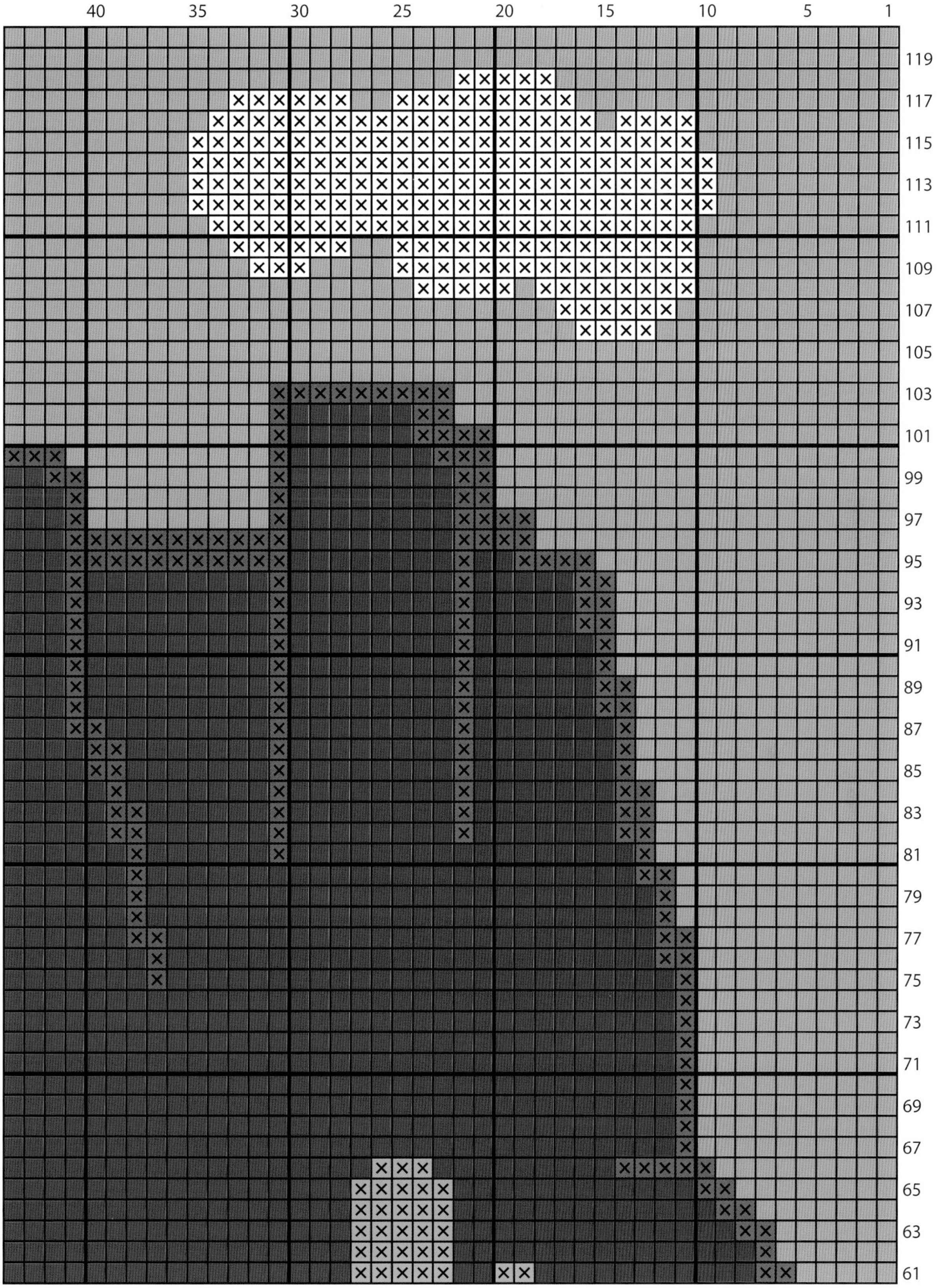

Grand Teton Paw Print Picnic Roll

Krista Ann

There are hundreds of grizzly bears who call Grand Teton National Park home, including the world's most famous bear, Grizzly 399, who mothered at least twenty-two cubs. A possible sighting of these incredibly massive creatures is one big reason that people visit this gorgeous park. Stitch up your own picnic roll, pack a lunch, and head out to your favorite scenic spot for a hike and meal with a view. Who knows what wildlife you will see!

Grizzly 399 with one of her cubs, roaming Grand Teton National Park.

DIFFICULTY LEVEL

Easy

FINISHED SIZE

14" (35.5 cm) tall and 16¼" (41 cm) long, not including tie closure.

YARN

Worsted Weight (#4 Medium)

Shown in: Lion Brand 24/7 Cotton (100% Mercerized Cotton; 186 yd [170 m]/3.5 oz [100 g]): Bear Paw Prints version: #098C Ecru (MC), 2 balls, and #126AA Café Au Lait (CC), 1 ball; Striped version: #098C Ecru (MC), 1 ball, and #126AA Café Au Lait (CC), 1 ball.

HOOK

Size F (3.75 mm).

Adjust hook size as needed to obtain gauge.

NOTIONS

Markers (m); scissors; tapestry needle for weaving in ends and cross-stitching graphic.

GAUGE

18 sts × 22 rows in Single Crochet Stitch = 4" (10 cm).

NOTES

Two versions of this picnic roll are provided, one accented with paw prints and the other with simple stripes. The paw prints are added using cross stitch.

Once finished, fold piece in half longways and then in half the other way to create a smaller rectangle. Roll from right to left and wrap longer tie closure around piece twice and close with a loose knot.

continued →→

Bear Paw Prints INSTRUCTIONS

With MC, ch 73.

Setup Row: Sc in 2nd ch from hook and in each ch across, turn—72 sc.

Row 1: Ch 1, sc in each st across, turn.

Rep Row 1 until you have worked a total of 70 rows. Do not fasten off.

Border

Ch 1, hdc in next 71 sts, 3 hdc in last st; working in ends of rows along the side edge, * hdc in end of next row, hdc2tog (over ends of next 2 rows); rep from * to next corner. 3 hdc in corner; working along opposite side of foundation ch, hdc in next 71 ch, 3 hdc in last ch; working in ends of rows along the side edge, ** hdc in end of next row, hdc2tog (over ends of next 2 rows); rep from ** to last corner, 3 hdc in corner; join with sl st in first hdc.

Fasten off.

Cross Stitch

Following Paw Print Chart, cross stitch bear paw prints onto picnic roll with CC.

Weave in any rem tails.

Tie Closure

With MC, ch 4.

Setup Row: Hdc in 2nd ch from hook and next 2 ch, turn—3 hdc.

Row 1: Ch 1, hdc in next 3 sts, turn.

Rep Row 1 until tie measures 23" (58.5 cm) long. Do not fasten off.

With RS of picnic roll facing toward you. Place a marker about a quarter of the way down the left-hand side of roll. Hold the last row of tie closure parallel with picnic roll so that the marker is aligned with the center st on tie closure. Hdc in next 3 sts on both the tie closure and the picnic roll, turn.

Rep Row 1 until tie measures 6" (15 cm) from where it was attached to the picnic roll. Fasten off.

Weave in any rem tails. Block piece to measurements.

continued →→

Paw Print Chart

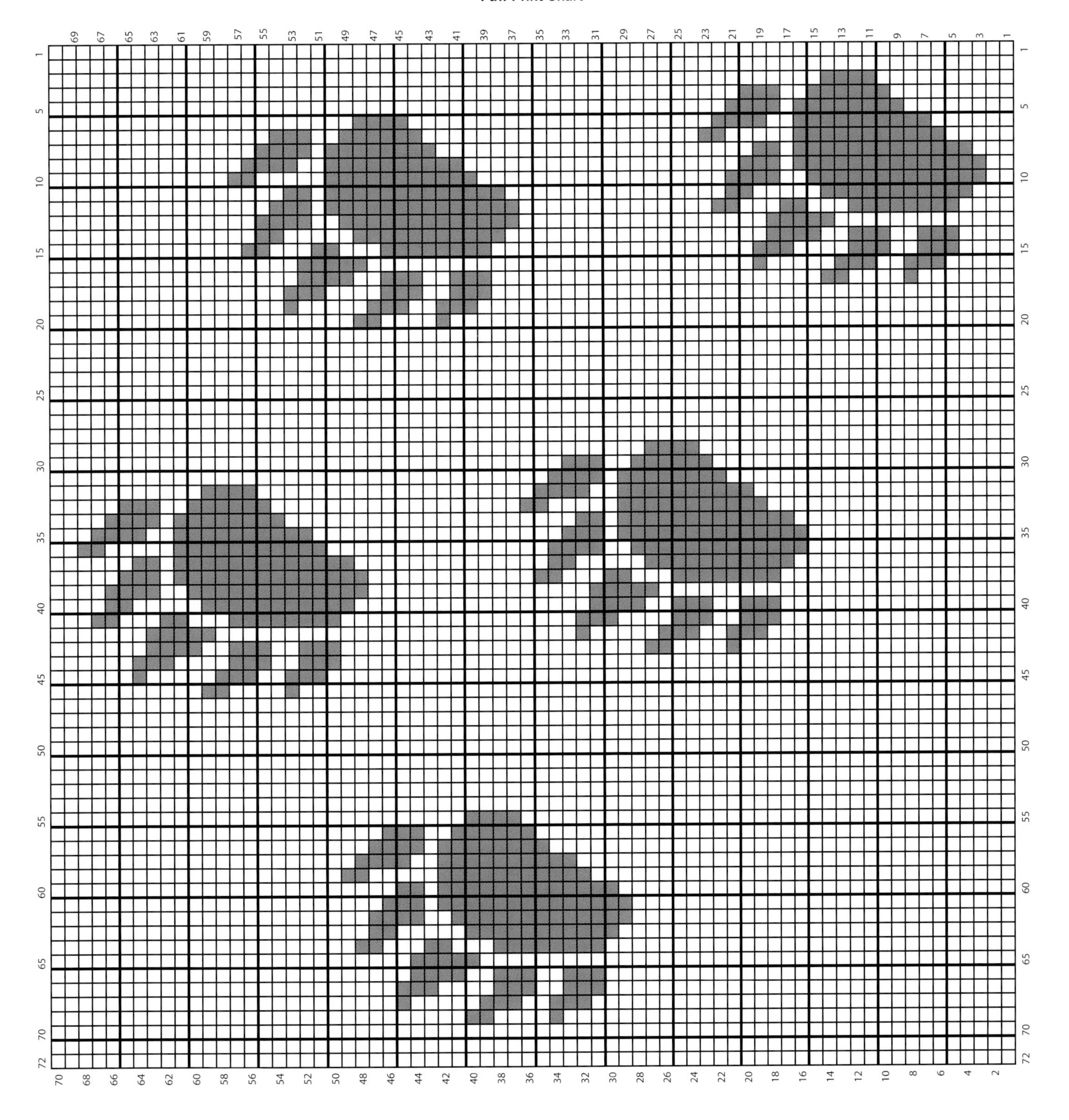

Striped INSTRUCTIONS

With MC, ch 73.

Setup Row: With MC, sc in 2nd ch from hook and in each ch across, turn—72 sc.

Row 1: With MC, ch 1, sc in each st across, turn.

Rep Row 1 until you have worked a total of 8 rows worked with MC.

Change to CC. Fasten off MC.

With CC, rep Row 1 for 8 rows.

Change to MC. Fasten off CC.

With MC, rep Row 1 for 8 rows.

Change to CC. Fasten off MC.

Rep last 16 rows until you have a total of 9 stripes. (5 MC stripes and 4 CC stripes). Do not fasten off MC after last stripe. Work Border and Tie Closure instructions from Bear Paw Prints version to complete the mat.

Block piece to measurements.

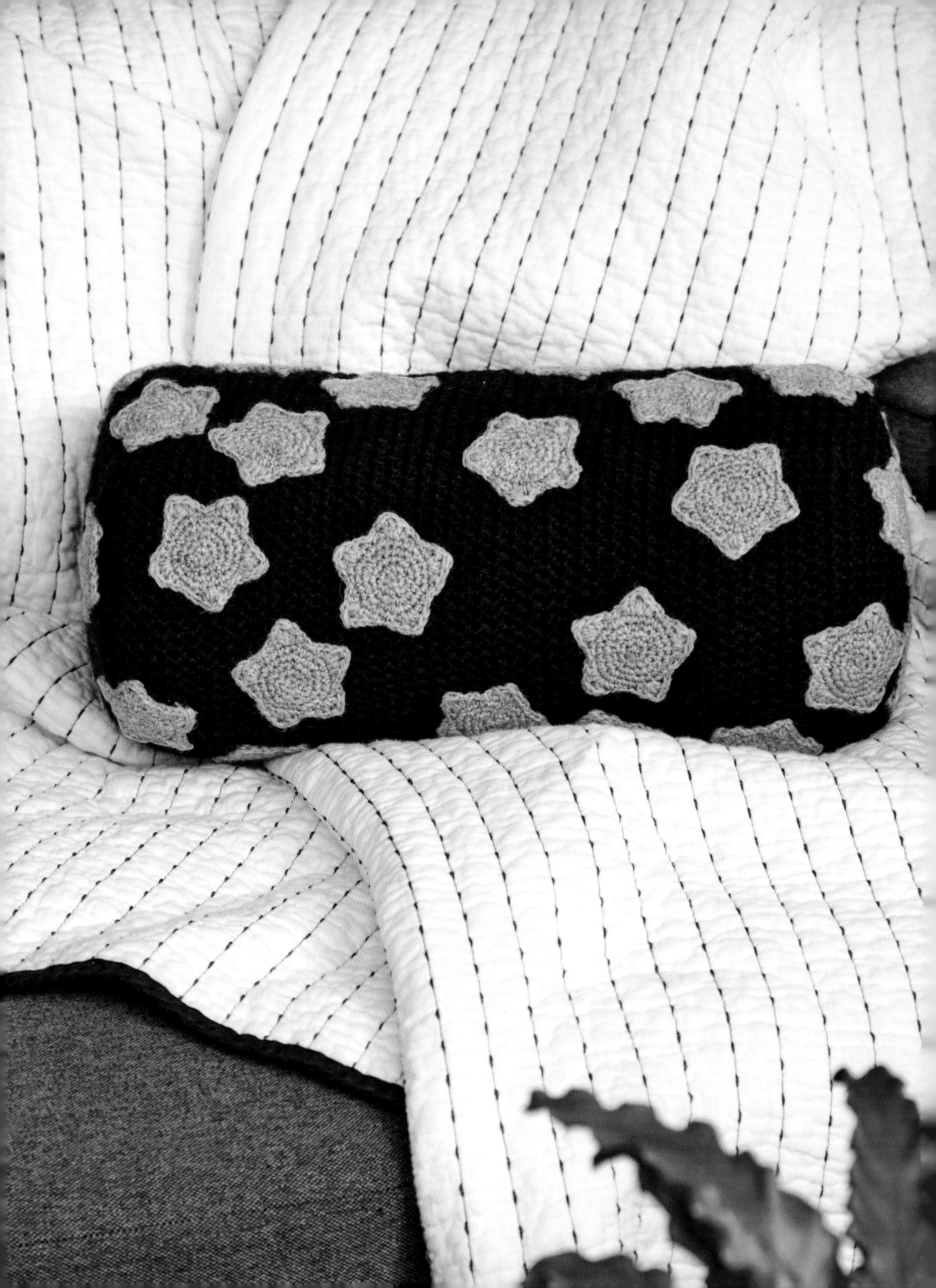

Great Basin Stargazing Pillow

Krista Ann

Great Basin National Park is remotely located in eastern Nevada where there are no major cities within miles. This remoteness makes it a spectacular place for star watching. During the summer months, the Milky Way hangs in the sky for stargazers and astro-photographers to enjoy. Grab a blanket and your newly crocheted pillow and head out into the darkness to lie down and absorb the night sky in all its glory.

Stargazers in the Great Basin can see spectacular views of the Milky Way on cloudless nights.

DIFFICULTY LEVEL

Easy

FINISHED SIZE

Approximately 17" (43 cm) long, 8" (20.5 cm) diameter measures, and 24" (61 cm) circumference.

YARN

Stars

DK Weight (#3 Light)

Shown in: Knit Picks Wool of the Andes Sport (100% Peruvian Highland Wool; 137 yd [125 m]/1.76 oz [50 g]: #25656 Dove Heather (C1), 3 balls.

Pillowcase

Worsted Weight (#4 Medium)

Shown in: Knit Picks Wool of the Andes (100% Peruvian Highland Wool; 110 yd [100 m]/1.76 oz [50 g]: #25640 Midnight Heather (C2), 4 balls.

HOOKS

Size E/4 (3.50 mm) for the stars.

Size I/9 (5.50 mm) for the pillowcase.

Adjust hook size as needed to obtain gauge.

GAUGE

15 sts × 11½ rnds in Half Double Crochet Stitch = 4" (10 cm) with larger hook.

NOTIONS

Locking stitch markers (m); scissors; tapestry needle; small "crib-size" Poly-fil quilt batting measuring 45" × 60" (114 × 152.5 cm); old black t-shirt (optional); dark-colored sewing thread (optional); sewing needle (optional).

NOTES

Stars are worked first and then set aside to be blocked and dry while pillowcase is made. Pillowcase is worked in the round. Poly-fil quilt batting is folded and rolled up to be used as the form for inside the pillowcase.

Make as many stars as you would like to add to the pillow. The sample shown has 48 stars. Additional stars may require more yarn.

continued →→

Pillow INSTRUCTIONS

Stars

Notes: When working the stars, leave a 6" (15 cm) beg tail and a 20" (51 cm) ending tail. The tails will be used to attach the stars after blocking.

Rnd 1: With C1, make a magic ring, ch 1 (counts as first sc), 5 sc in ring; join with sl st to beg-ch—6 sts.

Pull on beg tail to close magic ring.

You will now be making a spiral with no chains at the bor or sl st at the end of the rnds.

Place a marker on the first sc worked in Rnd 2 to indicate the bor. Move marker up as each rnd is worked.

Rnd 2: Work 2 sc in same st as joining sl st, 2 sc in next 5 sts—12 sts.

Rnd 3: *2 sc in next st, sc in next st; rep from * around—18 sts.

Rnd 4: *2 sc in the next st, sc in next 2 sts; rep from * around—24 sts.

Rnd 5: *2 sc in the next st, sc in next 3 sts; rep from * around—30 sts.

Rnd 6: *Sc in next st, hdc in next st, (dc, trc, dc) in next st, hdc in next st, sc in next st, sl st in next st; rep from * around.

Cut yarn, leaving about a 20" (51 cm) tail for tacking star onto pillowcase.

Block all stars by soaking in water. Lay each star onto a blocking mat and pin so that the tips of each star are pulled out at each point. Let dry completely. Do not cut the beg or ending tails.

Pillowcase

Increase Rounds

Rnd 1: With C2, make a magic ring, ch 2 (counts as first hdc). 7 hdc in ring; join with sl st into beg-ch—8 sts.

Pull on beg tail to close magic ring.

Note: You will now be making a spiral with no chains at the bor or sl st at the end of the rnds.

Place a marker on the first sc worked in Rnd 2 to indicate the bor. Move marker up as each rnd is worked.

Rnd 2: 2 hdc in the next 8 sts—16 sts.

Rnd 3: *2 hdc in the next st, hdc in next st; rep from * around—24 sts.

Rnd 4: *2 hdc in the next st, hdc in next 2 sts; rep from * around—32 sts.

Rnd 5: *2 hdc in the next st, hdc in next 3 sts; rep from * around—40 sts.

Rnd 6: *2 hdc in the next st, hdc in next 4 sts; rep from * around—48 sts.

Rnd 7: *2 hdc in the next st, hdc in next 5 sts; rep from * around—56 sts.

Rnd 8: *2 hdc in the next st, hdc in next 6 sts; rep from * around—64 sts.

Rnd 9: *2 hdc in the next st, hdc in next 7 sts; rep from * around—72 sts.

Rnd 10: *2 hdc in the next st, hdc in next 8 sts; rep from * around—80 sts.

Rnd 11: *2 hdc in the next st, hdc in next 9 sts; rep from * around—88 sts.

Rnd 12: *2 hdc in the next st, hdc in next 10 sts; rep from * around—96 sts.

Work Even

Keep bor marker in place to indicate where increase rnds end. Work hdc in every stitch around and around until piece measures 13½" (34.5 cm) from marker.

Decrease Rounds

Rnd 1: *hdc2tog, hdc in next 10 sts; rep from * around—88 sts.

Rnd 2: *hdc2tog, hdc in next 9 sts; rep from * around—80 sts.

Rnd 3: *hdc2tog, hdc in next 8 sts; rep from * around—72 sts.

Turn pillowcase inside out and weave in any tails. Turn right side out. Roll quilt batting into a cylinder shape and stuff it into your pillowcase. Finish out the decrease rnds closing the form into the pillowcase.

Note: If you are working with a darker-colored yarn and your quilt batting is white, take an old black t-shirt or black stretchy fabric and wrap the fabric around the quilt batting. Lightly sew the fabric in place so that the quilt batting is completely covered in black fabric.

Rnd 4: *hdc2tog, hdc in next 7 sts; rep from * around—64 sts.

Rnd 5: *hdc2tog, hdc in next 6 sts; rep from * around—56 sts.

Rnd 6: *hdc2tog, hdc in next 5 sts; rep from * around—48 sts.

Rnd 7: *hdc2tog, hdc in next 4 sts; rep from * around—40 sts.

Rnd 8: *hdc2tog, hdc in next 3 sts; rep from * around—32 sts.

Rnd 9: *hdc2tog, hdc in next 2 sts; rep from * around—24 sts.

Rnd 10: *hdc2tog, hdc in next st; rep from * around—16 sts.

Rnd 11: *hdc2tog; rep from * around—8 sts.

Cut yarn, leaving a tail. Weave tail through sts of Rnd 11 and cinch tight to close the hole.

Finishing

Use the beg tail to tack down the stars and place them where you want around the pillow. Once all the stars are lightly tacked down with the beg tail, use the ending tail to sew the stars to the pillow. Weave in and trim all ends.

Katmai Grizzly Bear Cup Cozy

Angel Doherty

With more brown bears than people living on the Alaskan Peninsula, it is no wonder that Katmai National Park is the best place in the United States to witness these spectacular creatures. During the summer months, a brown bear can eat as many as thirty salmon in a single day. The park has safe places where you can watch the bears in their natural habitat as they gorge themselves on salmon. If you love bears as much as bears love fish, this is a project that will be a joy to stitch up!

Fat Bear Week is a popular annual tournament hosted by Katmai National Park in October that lets visitors and online viewers vote for the bear they think gained the most weight by eating the most fish ahead of hibernation!

DIFFICULTY LEVEL
Intermediate

FINISHED SIZE

5" (12.5 cm) tall, 5" (12.5 cm) wide, and 3" (7.5 cm) deep.

YARN

Worsted Weight (#4 Medium)

Shown in: Big Twist Value (100% Acrylic; 380 yd [347 m]/6 oz [170 g]): Chocolate Brown (MC) and Cream (C2), 1 skein of each.

Ice Yarns Eyelash (100% Polyester; 82 yd [75 m]/1.75 oz [50 g]): #22754 Dark Brown (C1), 1 ball.

Yarn Bee Soft Secret (100% Acrylic; 300 yd [274 m]/6 oz (170 g]): #38 Mist (C3), 1 skein.

HOOKS

Size E/4 (3.5 mm), H/8 (5.00 mm), and J/10 (6.00 mm).

Adjust hook size as needed to obtain gauge.

NOTIONS

Locking stitch marker (m); two 15 mm black shank buttons (for eyes); one 25 mm animal nose (or yarn to embroider a nose); scissors; tapestry needle; fiberfill; and slicker brush (optional).

GAUGE

Approximately 4 sts = 1" (2.5 cm) with largest hook.

NOTES

It can be tricky crocheting with furry yarns. You may need to crochet slower and with looser tension than usual. Gently guide your hook through the fur as you stitch. If you need to undo your work, take it one stitch at a time, pulling gently.

MC and C1 are held together throughout.

The fluff can get stuck inside your project when crocheting with eyelash yarns. To bring the fluff to the surface, you are going to give it a gentle brush with a wire slicker brush. A wire dog grooming brush works great for this. Brush the cozy base thoroughly in all directions, when completing each part of the cozy.

Safety eyes are not recommended because the posts would prevent the cozy base from lying flat on your cup. Take care while attaching the eyes. Placing them too high or too close together is a common mistake.

continued →→

Cozy INSTRUCTIONS

Cozy Base

Note: The cozy base is worked in continuous rounds (instead of joined rounds).

With MC and C1 held together and largest hook, ch 28. Join in a ring with sl st into the first ch, be careful not to twist the chain. Place m at first stitch of rnd and move as each rnd is completed.

Rnd 1: Sc in the same st as the sl st, sc in each st around —28 sc.

Rnds 2–10: Sc in each st around.

Note: Rnd 11 is rounded in the front of the cozy to create a forehead.

Rnd 11: 10 sc, hdc, 2 dc same st, dc, dc and trc same st, trc and dc same st, dc, 2 dc same st, hdc, 10 sc, sl st to first sc.

Fasten off and weave in tails. Set the cozy base aside.

Snout

Rnd 1: With C2 and middle-size hook, make a magic ring. Ch 1, make 6 sc in the ring, and continue to crochet in the round.

Place m at first stitch of rnd and move as each rnd is completed.

Rnd 2: 2 sc into each st around—12 sc.

Rnd 3: 2 sc in first st, 1 sc in next st, [2 sc in next st, sc in next st] around—18 sc.

Rnds 4–8: Sc in each st around.

Rnd 9: Sc in first 2 sts, 2 sc in next st, [sc in next 2 sts, 2 sc in next st] around—24 sc.

Rnd 10: Sc in each st around; join with sl st to first sc, fasten off, and leave a long tail for sewing onto the cozy base.

Attach the animal nose in the center of the snout. There will be a small hole in the center of the magic ring that makes this simple! You can also embroider a nose.

Attach the Snout to the Cozy Base

Position the cozy base with the forehead created in Rnd 11 centered in the front. Stuff the snout with a small amount of fiberfill. Place the snout on the first row of stitches, with the nose in the middle of the forehead. Sew onto the cozy using the long tail and tapestry needle. After attaching, weave in the tail.

Attach the Eyes

Position the eyes 6 sts apart, with the bottom of each eye just below the top of the snout. Sew on with needle and thread.

Ears (Make 2)

With 1 strand each of MC and C1 held together and largest hook, leave a 12" (30 cm) tail at the beg of your chain to use it to sew the ear onto the cozy base, ch 7.

Row 1: Sc in the 2nd ch from hook and in each ch across, turn—6 sc.

Row 2: Ch 1, sc in first 2 sts, sc2tog, sc in last 2 sts, turn—5 sc.

Row 3: Ch 1, sc in first 2 sts, sc2tog, sc in last st, turn—4 sc.

Row 4: Ch 1, sc in first st, sc2tog, sc in last st, turn—3 sc.

Row 5: Ch 1, sc in first st, hdc in next st, sc in last st, turn.

Fasten off and weave in tails at the top of the ear.

Attach the Ears

Place the ear on the top of the cozy with the tail end at the beg of the forehead sts. Angle ear, so the opposite side is between the top 2 rounds of the cozy base. Sew on using the yarn tail and a tapestry needle. Weave in ends.

Finishing the Cozy

Once you have attached both ears, gently brush the front, back, sides, and edges with the wire brush. Continue brushing until they are very fluffy. To shape the fur on the ears, trim the yarn using a sharp pair of scissors. It's best to take off small amounts at a time. During trimming, give the cozy a good shake to see where the yarn settles.

continued →→

Salmon INSTRUCTIONS

Body

Rnd 1: With C3 and smallest hook, make a magic ring, ch 1, make 4 sc in the ring, and continue to crochet in the round.

Place m at first stitch of rnd and move as each rnd is completed.

Rnd 2: Sc inc, 2 sc, sc inc—6 sc.

Rnd 3: Sc in each st around.

Rnd 4: Sc inc, 4 sc, sc inc—8 sc.

Rnd 5: Sc in each st around.

Rnd 6: 2 sc in next 2 sts, sc in next 6 sts—10 sc.

Rnds 7 and 8: Sc in each st around.

Rnd 9: 2 sc in first st, sc in next 8 sts, 2 sc in last st—12 sc.

Rnds 10–13: Sc in each st around.

Rnd 14: Sc2tog, sc in next 10 sts—11 sc.

Rnd 15: Sc in each st around.

Rnd 16: Sc2tog, sc in next 9 sts—10 sc.

Rnd 17: Sc in each st around.

Rnd 18: Sc2tog, sc in next 8 sts—9 sc.

Rnd 19: Sc in each st around.

Rnd 20: Sc2tog, sc in next 7 sts—8 sc.

Rnd 21: Sc2tog, sc in next 6 sts—7 sc.

Rnd 22: Sc in each st around.

You will be working in rows instead of rounds for the rest of the tail.

Row 23: Sl st in next st, ch 1 turn, squish the last round of the tail together. Inserting your hook through both layers, sc across, turn—3 sc.

Row 24: Ch 1, 2 sc in first st, sc in next st, 2 sc in last st, turn—5 sc.

Row 25: Ch 1, 2 sc in first st, sc in next 3 sts, 2 sc in last st, turn—7 sc.

Row 26: Ch 1, 2 sc in first st, sc in next 2 sts, sl st in next st, sc in next 2 sts, 2 sc in last st—9 sts.

Fasten off and weave in the tail.

Salmon Diagram

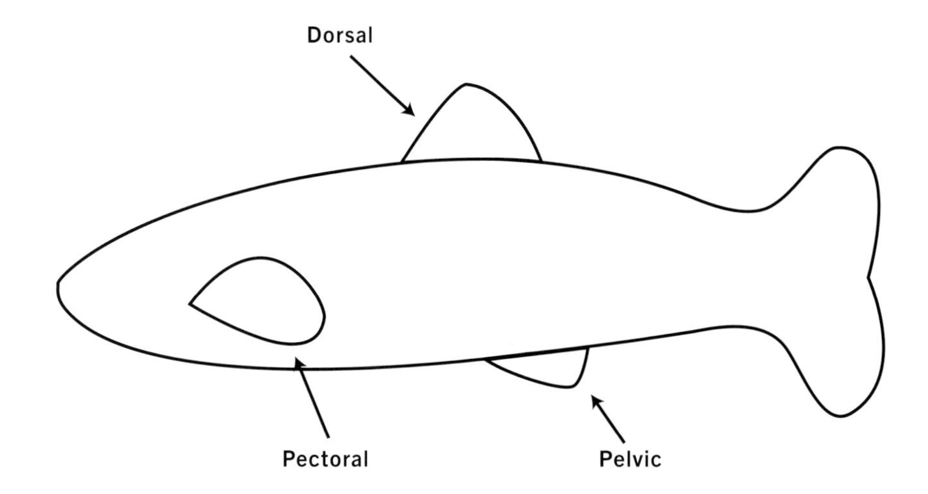

Dorsal Fin

Insert smallest hook through both layers at the top of the fish on Rnd 13, pull C3 through, ch 3, dc in the same space as the ch 3, and continue working through both layers towards the head, hdc, sl st. Fasten off and weave in tails.

Pectoral and Pelvic Fins (Make 2)

With C3 and smallest hook, ch 4.

Row 1: Sc in 2nd ch from hook, sc in next ch, sl st in last ch—3 sts.

Fasten off, leaving a tail to sew on.

Finishing the Salmon

Place the tail end of the pectoral fin on Rnd 4 of the body, and sew on 1 row up from the bottom of the fish using the tails. Weave in the rem ends.

Place the tail end of the pelvic fin on Rnd 12 of the body, and sew it onto the bottom row using the tails. Weave in the rem ends.

Embroider an eye between Rnds 1 and 2, one row down from the top of the fish.

Attach the Salmon to the Bear

Lower Jaw

With C2 and middle-size hook, ch 6, leaving a long tail at the beg to sew onto the cozy base.

Row 1: Sc in 2nd ch from hook and in each ch across, turn—5 sc.

Rows 2–6: Sc in each st across, turn.

Row 7: Sc in first 2 sts, sc2tog, sc in last st, turn—4 sc.

Row 8: Sc in first st, sc2tog, sc in last st, turn—3 sc.

Row 9: Sc in first st, hdc in next st, sc in last st—3 sts.

Fasten off, leaving a 12" (30 cm) tail to be used in a later step to secure the salmon in the bear's mouth.

Place the jaw with the bottom centered on the bottom of the snout, and sew it on using the tail from the beg chain. Weave in the ends. Weave in the top tail from the top of the jaw to the middle of row 7. Keep the tapestry needle on the yarn end.

Place the salmon inside the lower jaw with all the fins showing on the outside of the mouth. Insert the tapestry needle through the salmon and the snout until it's inside the cozy base.

Go back through the snout, salmon, and to the front of the jaw. Go back through the jaw, salmon, and snout to the inside of the cozy base. This will close the lower jaw, and secure the salmon. Weave in the ends.

Olympic Grand Fir Fingerless Mitts

Brenda K. B. Anderson

Olympic National Park is home to enormous trees, many the largest of their kind in North America, and some estimated to be more than 1,000 years old. The tallest tree in the park, a grand fir, measures an incredible 246 feet (75 m) tall! These fingerless mitts are an homage to these breathtaking trees, a reminder of their quiet, majestic beauty.

Abies grandis, or grand fir trees, are native to North America and are the largest trees in the "Forest of Giants."

DIFFICULTY LEVEL
Experienced

FINISHED SIZES

Adult S (M, L)

Finished circumference: 7¼" (7¾", 8½") [18.5 (19.5, 21.5) cm] circumference, not including thumb gusset (measured above or below).

Finished length: 9" (9¼", 9½") [23 (23.5, 24) cm]

Sample shown is size S. Choose a size that is closest to hand measurement.

YARN

Fingering Weight (#1 Super Fine)

Shown in: Cascade Heritage (75% Superwash Merino Wool, 25% Nylon; 437 yd [400 m]/3.5 oz [100 g]): #5612 Moss, 1 hank (for any size).

HOOKS

Size C/2 (2.75 mm).

Adjust hook size as needed to obtain gauge.

NOTIONS

Removeable st markers; tapestry needle.

GAUGE

25.5 sts in Extended Single Crochet (esc) × 24 rnds = 4" (10 cm).

NOTES

When working the cable pattern, it is helpful to look at the chart as well as the written directions.

There are times when sts are worked twice; once around the post and also in the top of the st.

There are also times when decrease sts are made. Some of the decrease sts also sk a st between the two sts that are worked. This happens whenever there are two different sts combined in one decrease st. For example, the FPtr-esc-dec, the esc-FPtr-dec, the FPtr-FPdc-dec and the FPdc-FPtr-dc sts. The only decrease st that does not sk a st between legs of the decrease is the dc3tog decrease.

The decreases and increases (where the sts are worked twice) always balance each other out in each rnd, so the st count always remains the same (17 sts across cable pattern).

To clarify the location for some post sts, st markers will be placed in the previous rnd as a placeholder. Leave markers in place until sts have been made *around the posts* of the marked sts. In many cases, sts will be worked in the top of the marked sts as well as around the posts.

STITCH GUIDE

Extended single crochet (esc): Insert hook in next st, yo and pull up lp, yo and pull through 1 lp, yo and pull through 2 lps.

Front post double crochet (FPdc): Yo, insert hook from front to back to front around the post of indicated st, yo and pull up lp, (yo and pull through 2 lps) twice.

Front post treble crochet (FPtr): Yo twice, insert hook from front to back to front around the post of indicated st, yo and pull up lp, (yo and pull through 2 lps) 3 times.

Front post treble/extended single crochet decrease (FPtr-esc-dec): Yo twice, insert hook from front to back to front around the post of the next st, yo and pull up lp, (yo and pull through 2 lps) twice, sk next st, insert hook in

continued →→

following st, yo and pull up lp, yo and pull through 1 lp, yo and pull though all 3 lps on hook.

Extended single crochet/Front post treble crochet decrease (Esc-FPtr-dec): Insert hook in next st, yo and pull up lp, yo and pull through 1 lp, yo twice, sk next st, insert hook from front to back to front around the post of the following st, yo and pull up lp, (yo and pull through 2 lps) twice, yo and pull though all 3 lps on hook.

Front post double crochet 3 sts together (FPdc3tog): *Yo, insert hook from front to back to front around the post of indicated st, yo and pull up lp, yo and pull through 2 lps; rep from * twice more (working around the posts of each of the next 2 sts), yo and pull through all 4 lps on hook.

Front post treble crochet/Front post double crochet decrease (FPtr-FPdc-dec): Yo twice, insert hook from front to back to front around the post of indicated st, yo and pull up lp, (yo and pull through 2 lps) twice, yo, sk next st, insert hook from front to back to front around the post of the following post st, yo and pull up lp, yo and pull through 2 lps, yo and pull though all 3 lps on hook.

Front post double crochet/Front post treble crochet decrease (FPdc-FPtr-dec): Yo, insert hook from front to back to front around the post of the next post st, yo and pull up lp, yo and pull through 2 lps, sk next st, yo twice, insert hook from front to back to front around the post of the following post st, yo and pull up lp, (yo and pull through 2 lps) twice, yo and pull though all 3 lps on hook.

GRAND FIR CABLE PATTERN (17 STS, 36 RNDS, EXCLUDING SET-UP RND)

Note: The following instructions are the written instructions for the *cable* pattern. These instructions are to be used in conjunction with the cable chart. To begin working the mitts, see "Mitt Instructions" section.

Rnds 1 and 2: Esc in each st around.

Rnds 3–11: Esc in each of next 7 sts, FPdc in next 3 sts, esc in each of next 7 sts. When working Rnd 11, place removeable marker in post of 1st, 2nd, 16th, and 17th sts of cable patt. On the following rnd, remove these markers only when you have worked around the posts of these marked sts.

Rnd 12: Esc in each of next 2 sts, FPtr in first marked post, FPtr-esc-dec starting with first leg made in next marked post, esc in each of next 3 sts, FPdc in each of next 3 sts, esc in each of next 3 sts, esc-FPtr-dec with the second leg of this st worked around the next marked post, FPtr in next marked post, esc in each of last 2 sts (in the top of the same 2 sts that have just been worked).

Rnd 13: Esc in each of next 4 sts, pm in post of each of the first 2 esc made, FPtr in first post st, FPtr-esc-dec starting with first leg made in next esc-FPtr-dec st, esc in next st, FPdc in each of next 3 sts, esc in next st, esc-FPtr-dec with the second leg of this st worked around the next esc-FPtr-dec, FPtr in next post st, esc in each of last 4 sts of cable patt (the first 2 esc are worked in the tops of sts that were already worked), pm in each of last 2 esc made.

Rnd 14: Esc in each of next 2 sts, FPtr in first marked post, FPtr-esc-dec starting with first leg made in next marked post, esc in each of next 2 sts, FPtr in next post st, FPtr-FPdc-dec with first leg worked in next FPtr-esc-dec, FPdc in next st, FPdc-FPtr-dec with second leg of st worked around esc-FPtr-dec, FPtr in next post st, esc in top of same esc-FPtr-dec, esc in next st, esc-FPtr-dec with second leg worked around next marked post, FPtr around following marked post, esc in the top of each of last 2 sts of cable pattern (the same 2 sts that have just been worked in).

Rnd 15: Esc in each of next 4 sts, pm in post of each of the first 2 esc made, FPtr in first post st, FPtr-esc-dec starting with first leg made in next esc-FPtr-dec st, esc in next st, FPdc in next post st (the top of this st has already been worked), FPdc3tog, FPdc in next post st, esc in top of the same post st that you just worked around, esc-FPtr-dec with the second leg made in next esc-FPtr-dec, FPtr in next post st, esc in post of each of last 4 sts of cable patt (the first 2 esc are worked in the tops of sts that were already worked), pm in each of last 2 esc made.

Rnds 16–19: Rep Rnds 14 and 15 twice more.

Rnd 20: Rep Rnd 14.

Rnd 21: Rep Rnd 15 but DO NOT place any markers.

Rnd 22: Esc in each of next 6 sts, pm in post of the 3rd and 4th of these esc, FPtr in next post st, FPtr-FPdc-dec with first leg worked in FPtr-esc-dec, FPdc in next st, FPdc-FPtr-dec with second leg of st worked around esc-FPtr-dec, FPtr in next post st, esc in each of last 6 sts of cable patt (the first esc are worked in the tops of sts that were already worked), pm in posts of the first and second of these 4 esc.

Rnd 23: Esc in each of next 4 sts, FPtr in first marked post, FPtr-esc-dec starting with first leg made in next marked post, esc in next st, FPdc in next post st (the top of this st has already been worked), FPdc3tog, FPdc in next post st, esc in the top of the same post st that you just worked around, esc-FPtr-dec with the second leg of this st worked around the next marked post, FPtr in next marked post st, esc in each of last 4 sts of cable patt (the first 2 esc are worked in the tops of sts that were already worked).

Rnds 24–27: Rep Rnds 22 and 23 twice more.

Rnd 28: Rep Rnd 22 but DO NOT place any markers.

Rnd 29: Esc in each of next 7 sts, pm in posts of 5th and 6th of these esc, FPdc in next post st (the top of this st has already been worked), FPdc3tog, FPdc in next post st, esc in each of last 7 sts of cable patt (the first esc is worked in the top of a st that was already worked), pm in post of the first and second of these 6 esc.

Rnd 30: Esc in each of next 6 sts, FPtr in next marked post, FPtr-FPdc-dec with first leg worked in next marked post, FPdc in next st, FPdc-FPtr-dec with second leg of st worked around next marked post, FPtr in next marked post, esc in each of next 6 sts (the first 2 of these sts are made in the tops of sts that were already worked).

Rnds 31 and 32: Rep Rnds 29 and 30.

Rnd 33: Rep Rnd 29 but DO NOT place any markers.

Rnd 34: Esc in each of the next 7 sts, FPdc in each of next 3 sts, esc in each of next 7 sts.

Rnd 35: Esc in each of next 8 sts, FPdc3tog with a leg around each of the 3 post sts, esc in the top of the same st as last leg of FPdc3tog just made, esc in each of next 7 sts.

Rnd 36: Esc in each of the next 8 sts, FPdc in next st, esc in each of next 8 sts.

continued →→

Mitt INSTRUCTIONS

Ribbed Cuff

Ch 8.

Row 1: Working in the bottom of chain, hdc in 2nd ch from hook and in each ch across, turn—7 sts.

Rows 2–38 (42, 48): Ch 1, hdc BLO in each st across, turn.

Joining: Fold cuff so that foundation ch is directly behind last row worked. Working through both thicknesses, ch 1, sl st BLO in each st across.

Turn sl st seam to inside of work, do not fasten off.

Using markers, divide ribbing in 4 equal sections. Begin by placing a marker on the working lp, then one directly opposite working lp (cuff is now divided in half). Then add one marker halfway between markers (cuff is now divided evenly in 4 sections).

Right Mitt

Setup rnd: Ch 1, working in ends of rows along edge of cuff, work 12 (13, 14) esc in each section, do not join, but continue in spiral rnds—48 (52, 56) sts.

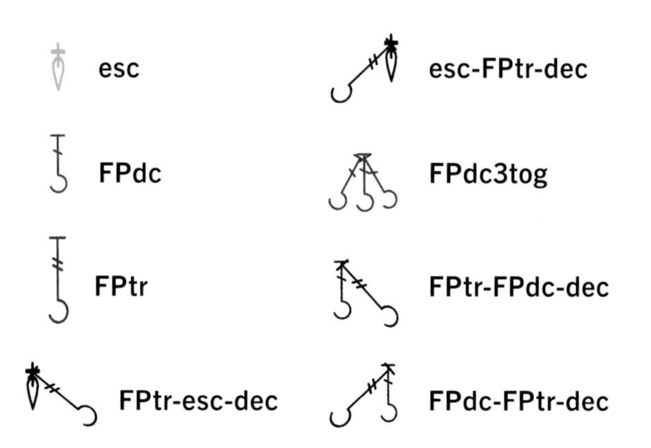

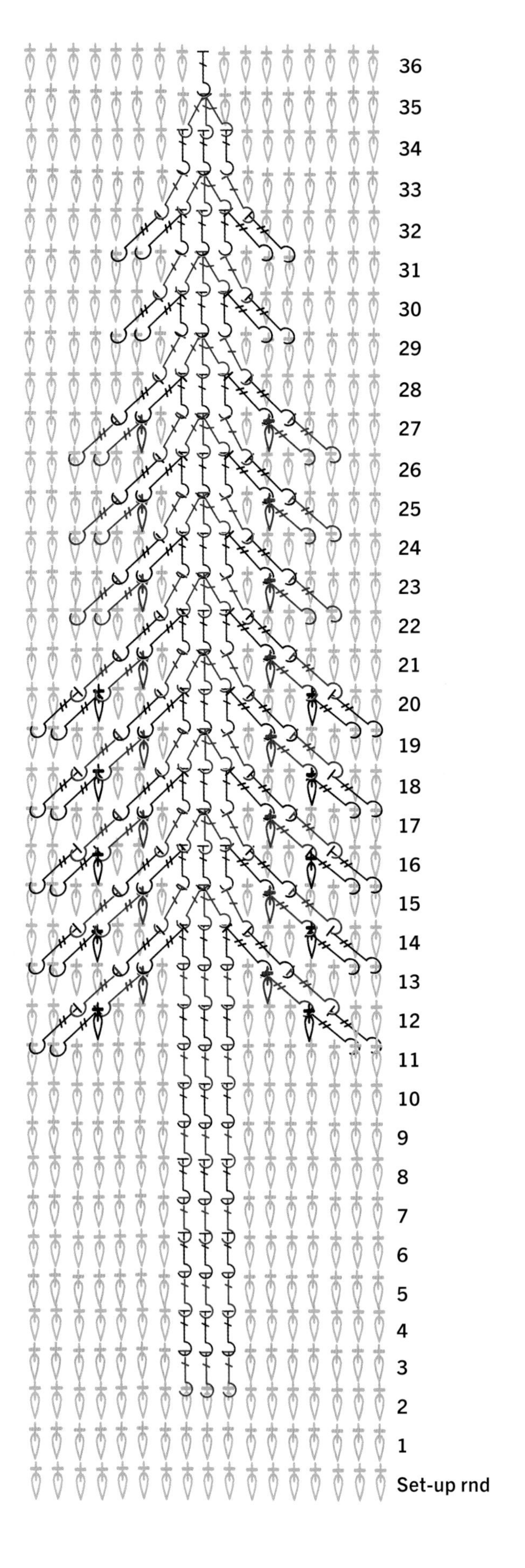

Remove all markers, then place a marker in the first st to indicate the bor. Move marker up as each rnd is worked.

Rnds 1 and 2: Esc in each st around.

Note: The cable pattern will be worked starting with the 4th (5th, 6th) st of the rnd and ending with the 20th (21st, 22nd) st of the rnd. You may wish to mark these sts with contrasting markers to keep track of the location for the 17 sts of the cable pattern.

Rnd 3–11: Esc in each of next 10 (11, 12) sts, FPdc in each of next 3 sts, esc in each of rem 35 (38, 41) sts. When working Rnd 11, place removeable marker in post of 4th (5th, 6th), 5th (6th, 7th), 19th (20th, 21st), and 20th (21st, 22nd) st of rnd.

Rnd 12: Esc in each of the next 3 (4, 5) sts, work cable/chart Rnd 12 over next 17 sts, esc in rem 28 (31, 34) sts. The post sts made in this rnd should be placed around the marked posts from prev rnd. Markers can be removed after a post st has been worked around the marked post.

Rnds 13–22: Esc in each of the next 3 (4, 5) sts, work next cable/chart rnd over next 17 sts, esc in rem 28 (31, 34) sts.

Increase for Thumb Gusset

Rnd 23: Esc in each of the next 3 (4, 5) sts, work Rnd 23 of cable/chart over next 17 sts, esc in next 5 (6, 7) sts, 2 esc in next st, esc in next st, pm in st just made to mark center of thumb gusset, 2 esc in next st, esc in rem 20 (22, 24) sts—2 sts inc, 50 (54, 58) sts.

Rnds 24–29: Esc in each of the next 3 (4, 5) sts, work next cable/chart rnd over next 17 sts, esc to 1 st before marked st, 2 esc in next st, esc in marked st (replace m in st), 2 esc in next st, esc in each st around—2 sts inc per rnd, 62 (66, 70) sts after working Rnd 29.

Rnd 30: Esc in each of the next 3 (4, 5) sts, work next cable/chart rnd over next 17 sts, esc in each st to end.

For sizes M (L) only:

Rnds 31 and 32: Rep Rnds 29 and 30—68 (72) sts. Note: From this point onward, the rnd number of the chart will not match the rnd of the mitt directions. For example, on the rnd that follows, you will be working across Rnd 31 of the chart, however you will be working Rnd 33 of your mitt.

For all sizes:

Rnd 31 (33, 33): Rep Rnd 29, working across Rnd 31 of the chart—64 (70, 74) sts.

Rnd 32 (34, 34)-35 (37, 37): Rep Rnd 30 for 4 times.

Rnd 36 (38, 38) (dividing for the thumb): Esc in each of the next 3 (4, 5) sts, work next cable/chart rnd over next 17 sts, esc in next 6 (7, 8) sts, ch 1, sk next 17 (19, 19) sts (for thumb), pm in first skipped st, esc in each of the rem 21 (23, 25) sts—47 (51, 55) sts and 1 ch-1 sp, excluding sts set aside for thumb.

Rnds 37 (39, 39)-38 (40, 41): Esc in each st and ch-1 sp around—48 (52, 56) sts.

Rnd 39 (41, 42): Esc in each st until 4 sts remain, sc in each of next 3 sts, sl st in last st.

Fasten off.

Weave in ends.

Thumb

For sizes S (M) only:

Rnd 1: Leaving 8" (20.5 cm) beg tail, pull up lp in marked st at thumb, ch 1 (does not count as a st), esc in same st and in each of next 16 (18) sts, esc in the bottom of the ch where thumb meets hand, do not join but continue to work in spiral rnds—18 (20) sts.

Rnd 2: Esc in each st until 2 sts remain, sc in next st, sl st in last st.

Fasten off. Weave in ends, using beg tail to sew any holes closed where thumb meets hand.

For size L only:

Rnd 1: Leaving 8" (20.5 cm) beg tail, pull up lp in marked st at thumb, ch 1 (does not count as a st), esc in same st and in each of next 18 sts, esc in space before ch-1 where thumb meets hand, esc in bottom of ch-1, esc in space before 1st esc, do not join but continue to work in spiral rnds—22 sts.

Rnd 2: Esc in each st until 2 sts remain, sc in next st, sl st in last st.

Fasten off. Weave in ends, using beg tail to sew any holes closed where thumb meets hand.

continued →→

Ribbing for Finger Edge

Ch 6.

Row 1: Working in the bottom of chain, hdc in 2nd ch from hook and in each ch across, turn—5 sts.

Rows 2–38 (42, 48): Ch 1, hdc BLO in each st across, turn.

Joining: Fold ribbing so that foundation ch is directly behind last row worked. Working through both thicknesses, ch 1, sl st BLO in each st across.

Turn sl st seam to inside of work, do not fasten off.

Fasten off, leaving a long tail for sewing. Use st markers to "pin" ribbing in place around finger opening. Use a whip stitch to sew ribbing to finger opening.

Weave in ends.

Ribbing for Thumb Edge

Ch 6.

Row 1: Working in the bottom of chain, hdc in 2nd ch from hook and in each ch across, turn—5 sts.

Rows 2–14 (16, 16): Ch 1, hdc BLO in each st across, turn.

Joining: Fold ribbing so that foundation ch is directly behind last row worked. Working through both thicknesses, ch 1, sl st BLO in each st across.

Fasten off, leaving a long tail for sewing. Turn sl st seam to inside of ribbing, use st markers to "pin" ribbing in place around thumb opening. Use a whip stitch to sew ribbing to thumb opening.

Weave in ends.

Left Mitt

Work Ribbed cuff same as for Right Mitt.
Work directions same as for Right Mitt through Rnd 22.

Increase for Thumb Gusset

Rnd 23: Esc in each of the next 3 (4, 5) sts, work Rnd 23 of cable/chart over next 17 sts, esc in next 24 (27, 30) sts (4 sts rem), 2 esc in next st, esc in next st, pm in st just made to mark center of thumb gusset, 2 esc in next st, esc in last st of rnd—2 sts inc, 50 (54, 58) sts.

Rnds 24–29: Rep Rnds 24–29 for Right Mitt.

Rnd 30: Esc in each of the next 3 (4, 5) sts, work next cable/chart rnd over next 17 sts, esc in each st to end.

For sizes M (L) only:

Rnds 31 and 32: Rep Rnds 29 and 30—68 (72) sts. Note: From this point onward, the round number of the chart will not match the rnd of the mitt directions. For example, on the round that follows, you will be working across Rnd 31 of the chart, however you will be working Rnd 33 of your mitt.

For all sizes:

Rnd 31 (33, 33): Repeat Rnd 29, working across Rnd 31 of the chart—64 (70, 74) sts.

Rnd 32 (34, 34)–35 (37, 37): Esc in each of the next 3 (4, 5) sts, work next cable/chart rnd over next 17 sts, esc in each st to end.

Rnd 36 (38, 38) (dividing for the thumb): Esc in each of the next 3 (4, 5) sts, work next cable/chart rnd over next 17 sts, esc in next 25 (28, 31) sts, ch 1, sk next 17 (19, 19) sts (for thumb), pm in first skipped st, esc in each of the rem 2 sts of rnd—47 (51, 55) sts and 1 ch-1 sp. excluding sts set aside for thumb.

Rnds 37 (39, 39)–38 (40, 41): Esc in each st and ch-1 sp around—48 (52, 56) sts.

Rnd 39 (41, 42): Esc in each st until 4 sts remain, sc in each of next 3 sts, sl st in last st.

Fasten off.

Weave in ends.

Work Thumb, Ribbing for Finger Edge, and Ribbing for Thumb Edge same as for Right Mitt.

Finishing

Weave in ends, block.

Petrified Forest Colors Cowl

Krista Ann

Cross-sections of petrified wood often display a gorgeous rainbow of colors. These shimmering hues of color are produced by different minerals present in water that seeps into the buried tree during the petrifying process. Much like the earth cloaks a fallen tree, which causes the petrification process to happen, this cowl will wrap around your neck and protect you from the elements.

The cross section of petrified trees reveals a rainbow of colors.

DIFFICULTY LEVEL

Easy

FINISHED SIZE

14½" (37 cm) tall, tube measures 24" (61 cm) in circumference, and tail of cowl measures 52" (132 cm) long.

YARN

DK Weight (#3 Light)

Shown in: Lion Brand Mandala (100% Acrylic; 590 yd [540 m]/5.3 oz [150g]): #204AW Chimera, 2 balls.

HOOKS

Size H/8 (5.00 mm) and I/9 (5.50 mm).

Adjust hook size as needed to obtain gauge.

NOTIONS

One 1¾" (44–45 mm) toggle button; scissors; tapestry needle.

GAUGE

16 sts in Primrose Stitch = 4" (10 cm) cm with smaller hook.

To make gauge swatch, use larger hook to ch 17. Switch to smaller hook and work Primrose Stitch (see Stitch Guide) until swatch measures a couple of inches.

STITCH GUIDE

Primrose Stitch Pattern (multiple of 3+2)

Chain a multiple of 3 plus 2 additional chains. (Example: 17 or 25 sts.)

Setup Row 1: (Sc, ch 2, sc) in 3rd ch from hook, * sk next 2 ch, (sc, ch 2, sc) in next ch; rep from * to last 2 ch, sk next ch, hdc in last ch, turn.

Row 1 (RS): Ch 3, 3 dc in each ch-2 sp across, dc in top of beg ch-2, turn.

Row 2: Ch 2, (sc, ch 2, sc) in center dc of each 3-dc group across, hdc in top of beg ch-3, turn.

Rep Rows 1 and 2 to establish the pattern.

continued →→

Cowl INSTRUCTIONS

With larger hook, ch 68.

Change to smaller hook.

Setup Row: (Sc, ch 2, sc) in 3rd ch from hook, * sk next 2 ch, (sc, ch 2, sc) in next ch; rep from * to last 2 ch, sk next ch, hdc in last ch, turn—44 sc and 22 ch-2 sps.

Row 1 (RS): Ch 3, 3 dc in each ch-2 sp across, dc in top of beg ch-2, turn—2 dc and 22 3-dc groups.

Row 2: Ch 2, (sc, ch 2, sc) in center dc of each 3-dc group across, hdc in top of beg ch-3, turn.

Rep Rows 1 and 2 until piece measures 24" (61 cm) from beg.

You will now be turning the flat work into a tube by working the next row together with the foundation ch.

Fold piece in half so RS is facing out, foundation ch is parallel to last row worked and each ch-2 space of the last row worked matches a foundation ch at the base of a (sc, ch 2, sc) group.

Joining Row: Sl st in first ch of foundation ch, ch 3, 3 dc in first ch-2 space of last row and in 3rd foundation ch, *sk to next ch-2 space, 3 dc in next ch-2 space and corresponding chain of foundation ch; rep from * across to beg ch-2, dc in beg ch-2 of last row and last ch of foundation ch, turn.

Rep Row 2.

Rep Rows 1 and 2 until piece measures approximately 52" (132 cm) from Joining Row. End after working a Row 2. Fasten off.

Weave in tails.

Placing Toggle Button

Lay cowl on a flat surface so that the tube is on the right and the tail of the cowl is on the left. Place cowl so that the foundation ch is under the fabric and not visible. In the bottom left corner of the tube, measure 3" (7.5 cm) in and 3" (7.5 cm) up from Joining Row. With a piece of scrap yarn, sew button securely to front layer of tube.

Redwood Tree Rings Coaster Set

Krista Ann

Walking through Redwood National Park among the trees is a gentle reminder how incredible our planet is and how tiny humans are. The tallest tree inside this park is a massive 380 feet (116 m) in height and is estimated to be over 600 years old. This park is arguably one of the most serene and majestic locations in the United States. There is no better place to grab your hook and yarn, find a place to sit, and stitch away in the shade created by the magnificent giant redwoods.

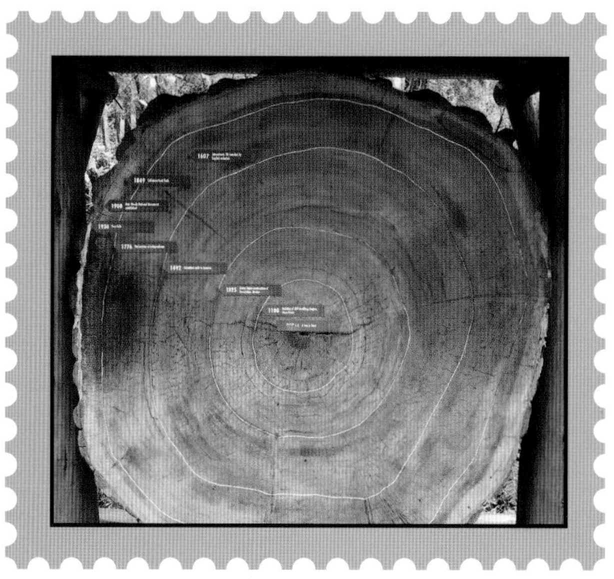

From the tree's birth more than 2,000 years ago to the signing of the US Declaration of Independence in 1776, the 1849 California Gold Rush, and the founding of Muir Woods in 1908, this tree lived through centuries of history before it fell in 1930.

DIFFICULTY LEVEL

Easy

FINISHED SIZE

Approximately 4" (10 cm) in diameter.

YARN

Worsted Weight (#4 Medium)

Shown in: Hobby Lobby I Love This Cotton (100% Cotton; 180 yd [165 m]/3.5 oz [100 g]): #95 Antique Cream (C1), #48 Taupe (C2), #80 Antique Gold (C3), and #20 Brown (C4), 1 ball of each.

HOOKS

Size I/9 (5.50 mm).

Adjust hook size as needed to obtain gauge.

NOTIONS

Locking stitch marker (m); scissors; tapestry needle.

GAUGE

18 sts in Single Crochet = 4" (10 cm).

NOTES

Like the rings of a real tree, each of these four coasters is unique. Feel free to follow the Color Sequences provided or mix things up for your own one-of-a-kind slice.

Always end with the darkest color to represent the bark of the tree.

To change yarn color, fasten off old color then join new color in any stitch of the last rnd worked.

continued →→

Coaster Set INSTRUCTIONS

Coaster (Make 4 – 1 in each Color Sequence in table)

Rnd 1: With first color in Color Sequence, make a magic ring, ch 1 (counts as first sc here and throughout), 5 sc in ring; join with sl st in beg-ch—6 sts.

Pull on beg tail to close magic ring. Continue to change yarn color following Color Sequence.

Rnd 2: Ch 1, sc in same st as joining sl st, 2 sc in next 5 sts; join with sl st in beg-ch—12 sts.

Rnd 3: Ch 1, sc in same st as joining sl st, sc in next st, *2 sc in next st, sc in next st; rep from * around; join with sl st in beg-ch—18 sts.

Rnd 4: Ch 1, sc in same st as joining sl st, sc in next 2 sts, *2 sc in next st, sc in next 2 sts; rep from * around; join with sl st in beg-ch—24 sts.

Rnd 5: Ch 1, sc in same st as joining sl st, sc in next 3 sts, *2 sc in next st, sc in next 3 sts; rep from * around; join with sl st in beg-ch—30 sts.

Rnd 6: Ch 1, sc in same st as joining sl st, sc in next 4 sts, *2 sc in next st, sc in next 4 sts; rep from * around; join with sl st in beg-ch—36 sts.

Rnd 7: Ch 1, sc in same st as joining sl st, sc in next 5 sts, *2 sc in next st, sc in next 5 sts; rep from * around; join with sl st in beg-ch—42 sts.

Rnd 8: Ch 1, sc in same st as joining sl st, sc in next 6 sts, *2 sc in next st, sc in next 6 sts; rep from * around; join with sl st in beg-ch—48 sts.

Rnd 9: Ch 1, sc in same st as joining sl st, sc in next 7 sts, *2 sc in next st, sc in next 7 sts; rep from * around; join with sl st in beg-ch—54 sts.

Rnd 10: Ch 1, hdc in same st as joining sl st, hdc in each rem st; join with sl st in beg-ch.

Fasten off.

Color Sequences	Coaster 1	Coaster 2	Coaster 3	Coaster 4
Rnd 1	C1	C2	C3	C1
Rnd 2	C1	C2	C3	C1
Rnd 3	C2	C3	C2	C2
Rnd 4	C3	C1	C1	C1
Rnd 5	C2	C1	C1	C3
Rnd 6	C2	C2	C3	C2
Rnd 7	C1	C3	C1	C1
Rnd 8	C3	C2	C3	C2
Rnd 9	C1	C3	C2	C2
Rnd 10	C4	C4	C4	C4

Finishing Coasters

Weave in all your tails. Lightly dampen coaster and lay on flat surface between two towels with a heavy book on top to flatten. Let dry overnight.

Coaster Holder

Rnds 1–9: With C4, work same as Rnds 1–9 of Coaster, do not change yarn color, work with C4 only—54 sts.

Rnd 10: Ch 1, sc in same st as joining sl st, sc in next 8 sts, *2 sc in next st, sc in next 8 sts; rep from * around; join with sl st in beg-ch—60 sts.

Rnd 11: Ch 1, sc in same st as joining sl st, sc in each rem st; join with sl st in beg-ch.

Rnd 12: Ch 1, hdc in same st as joining sl st, hdc in next 17 sts, hdc2tog, [hdc in next 18 sts, hdc2tog] twice; join with sl st in beg-ch—57 sts.

Rnd 13: Ch 3 (counts as dc), *sl in next st, dc in next st; rep from * around; join with sl st in top of beg-ch.

Rnd 14: *Dc in next st (this is the sl st from prev rnd), sl st in next st (this is the dc from prev rnd); rep from * around.

Fasten off and weave in tails.

Note: If you make more than 4 coasters, you can continue to repeat Rnd 14 to make your holder as tall as you need to fit all your coasters. You will work in a spiral with no ch sts at the bor. When desired height is reached, end with a sl st.

Rocky Mountain Mittens

Meghan Ballmer

Spanning over 3,000 miles (4828 km) from Canada to New Mexico, the Rockies are renowned for their stunning peaks, diverse wildlife, and breathtaking landscapes. These cozy mittens were inspired by the rugged beauty of the Rockies. Perfect for keeping your hands warm during chilly days, this pattern combines beautiful textures and classic stitches to create a pair of mittens that are both functional and stylish. Embrace the spirit of the Rocky Mountains and craft a pair of mittens that will become your go-to accessory for cold-weather adventures.

Snowmelt off the Rocky Mountains supplies nearly 40 million people in the Southwest with water.

DIFFICULTY LEVEL
Intermediate

FINISHED SIZE

9½" (24 cm) height and 4" (10 cm) width.

YARN

Worsted Weight (#4 Medium)

Shown in: Urth Yarn Harvest (100% Superwash Merino; 220 yd [200 m]/3.5 oz [100 g]): Walnut (MC), Grape Leaf (C1), Ecru (C2), Cosmic Purple Carrot (C3), 1 skein of each.

HOOKS

Size H (5.00 mm) and size G (4.25 mm).

Adjust hook size as needed to obtain gauge.

GAUGE

21 sts × 19 rnds in (sc in next st, FPsc) pattern stitch= 4" (10 cm).

NOTIONS

Stitch markers; scissors; tapestry needle; tape measure.

NOTES

Mittens are made bottom up starting with the cuff.

The cuff is made in rows and then seamed together to form a band.

The main body is worked directly into the cuff edges and is made in turned rounds.

Tapestry and/or intarsia crochet is used for the colorwork section.

continued →→

Mitten INSTRUCTIONS

Cuff

With C1 and larger hook, ch 10 leaving a long beg tail.

Row 1: Sl st in 2nd ch from hook and each ch across, turn—9 sts.

Rows 2–42: Ch 1, sl st BLO in each st across, turn.

Place a stitch marker in the working lp. Using the long tail from the beginning and a tapestry needle, seam the short ends of the cuff together using your preferred seaming method. Turn cuff RS out and continue to main body.

Main Body

Remove the stitch marker from the working lp and insert the smaller hook. With MC, yarn over and draw up a lp. Fasten off C1.

Work in turned rounds from here on.

Rnd 1 (RS): Sc into each row edge around; join with sl st in first st turn—42 sts.

Note: From here on, begin each rnd in stitch following the stitch the joining sl st was worked into.

Rnds 2–13: Ch 1, * sc in next st, FPsc around next st; rep from * around; join with sl st in first st, turn.

Right Mitten

Rnd 14: Ch 1, [sc in next st, FPsc around next st] twice, ch 7, sk next 7 sts (for thumb opening), FPsc around next st, * sc in next st, FPsc around next st; rep from * around; join with sl st in first st, turn.

Rnd 15: Ch 1, sc in next st, * FPsc around next st, sc in next st; rep from * to ch-7, sc in each ch of ch-7, [sc in next st, FPsc around next st] twice; join with sl st in first st, turn.

Rnds 16–21: Ch 1, * sc in next st, FPsc around next st; rep from * around; join with sl st in first st, turn.

Colorwork Section

For the colorwork, work in the (sc, FPsc) pattern stitch of previous rnds AND change yarn color using tapestry crochet and/or intarsia. Follow the chart OR the written instructions below. For Right Mitten, read even rows of chart from left to right and odd rows from right to left.

Written Instructions

Rnd 22 (WS): (MC) × 9, (C2) × 2, (MC) × 5, (C2) × 2, (MC) × 7, (C2) × 2, (MC) × 5, (C2) × 2, (MC) × 8

Rnd 23 (RS): * (MC) × 9, (C2) × 2, (MC) × 3, (C2) × 2; rep from * once more, (MC) × 10

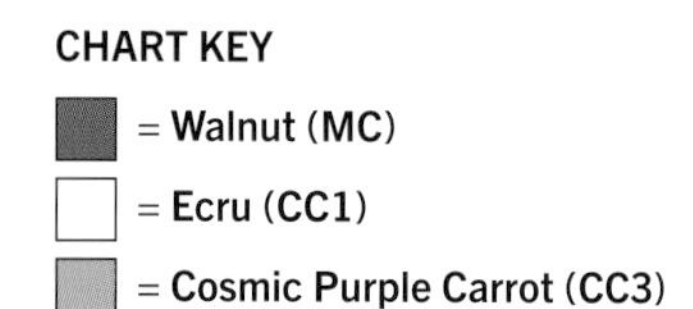

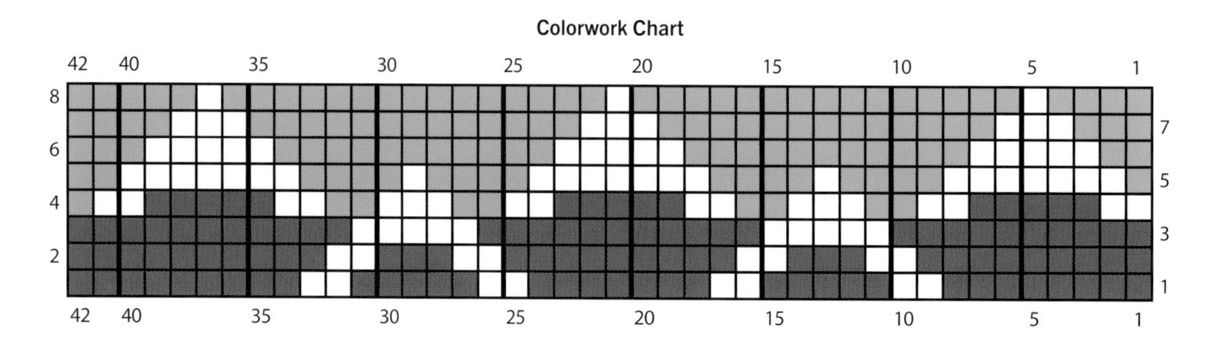

Rnd 24 (WS): * (MC) × 11, (C2) × 5; rep from * once more, (MC) × 10

Rnd 25 (RS): * (C2) × 2, (MC) × 5, (C2) × 2, (C3) × 2, (C2) × 3, (C3) × 2; rep from * once more, (C2) × 2, (MC) × 5, (C2) × 2, (C3) × 1

Rnd 26 (WS): (C3) × 2, * (C2) × 7, (C3) × 4, (C2) × 1, (C3) × 4; rep from * once more, (C2) × 7, (C3) × 1

Rnd 27 (RS): (C3) × 2, * (C2) × 5, (C3) × 11; rep from * once more, (C2) × 5, (C3) × 3

Rnd 28 (WS): (C3) × 4, * (C2) × 3, (C3) × 13; rep from * once more, (C2) × 3, (C3) × 3

Rnd 29 (RS): (C3) × 4, * (C2) × 1, (C3) × 15; rep from * once more, (C2) × 1, (C3) × 5

Left Mitten

Rnd 14: Ch 1, sc in next st, * FPsc around next st, sc in next st, rep from * to last 11 sts, ch 7, sk next 7 sts (for thumb opening), [sc in next st, FPsc around next st] twice; join with sl st in first st, turn.

Rnd 15: Ch 1, [sc in next st, FPsc around next st] twice, sc in each ch of ch-7, FPsc around next st, * sc in next st, FPsc around next st; rep from * around; join with sl st in first st, turn.

Rnds 16–21: Ch 1, * sc in next st, FPsc around next st; rep from * around; join with sl st in first st, turn.

Colorwork Section

For the colorwork, work in the (sc, FPsc) pattern stitch of previous rnds AND change yarn color using tapestry crochet and/or intarsia. Follow the chart OR the written instructions below. For Left Mitten, read even rows of chart from right to left and odd rows from left to right.

Written Instructions

Rnd 22 (RS): (MC) × 8, (C2) × 2, (MC) × 5, (C2) × 2, (MC) × 7, (C2) × 2, (MC) × 5, (C2) × 2, (MC) × 9

Rnd 23 (WS): (MC) × 10, * (C2) × 2, (MC) × 3, (C2) × 2, (MC) × 9; rep from * once more

Rnd 24 (RS): (MC) × 10, * (C2) × 5, (MC) × 11; rep from * once more

Rnd 25 (WS): (C3) × 1, * (C2) × 2, (MC) × 5, (C2) × 2, (C3) × 2, (C2) × 3, (C3) × 2; rep from * once more, (C2) × 2, (MC) × 5, (C2) × 2

Rnd 26 (RS): (C3) × 1, * (C2) × 7, (C3) × 4, (C2) × 1, (C3) × 4; rep from * once more, (C2) × 7, (C3) × 2

Rnd 27 (WS): (C3) × 3, * (C2) × 5, (C3) × 11; rep from * once more, (C2) × 5, (C3) × 2

Rnd 28 (RS): (C3) × 3, * (C2) × 3, (C3) × 13; rep from * once more, (C2) × 3, (C3) × 4

Rnd 29 (WS): (C3) × 5, * (C2) × 1, (C3) × 15; rep from * once more, (C2) × 1, (C3) × 4

Both Mittens – Shape Top of Mitten

With C3,

Rnd 30: Ch 1, sc in next st, [FPsc around next st, sc in next st] 4 times, sc3tog, [sc in next st, FPsc around next st] 9 times, sc3tog, FPsc around next st, [sc in next st, FPsc around next st] 4 times; join with sl st in first st, turn—38 sts.

Rnd 31: Ch 1, * sc in next st, FPsc around next st; rep from * around; join with sl st in first st, turn.

Rnd 32: Ch 1, [sc in next st, FPsc around next st] 4 times, sc3tog, [FPsc around next st, sc in next st] 8 time, sc3tog, [sc in next st, FPsc around next st] 4 times; join with sl st in first st, turn—34 sts.

Rnd 33: Ch 1, * sc in next st, FPsc around next st; rep from * around; join with sl st in first st, turn.

Rnd 34: Ch 1, sc in next st, [FPsc around next st, sc in next st] 3 times, sc3tog, [sc in next st, FPsc around next st] 7 times, sc3tog, FPsc around next st, [sc in next st, FPsc around next st] 3 times; join with sl st in first st, turn—30 sts.

Rnd 35: Ch 1, * sc in next st, FPsc around next st; rep from * around; join with sl st in first st, turn.

Rnd 36: Ch 1, [sc in next st, FPsc around next st] 3 times, sc3tog, [FPsc around next st, sc in next st] 6 times, sc3tog, [sc in next st, FPsc around next st] 3 times; join with sl st in first st, turn—26 sts.

Rnd 37: Ch 1, * sc in next st, FPsc around next st; rep from * around; join with sl st in first st, turn.

continued →→

Rnd 38: Ch 1, * sc2tog; rep from * around; join with sl st in first st, turn—13 sts.

Rnd 39: Ch 1, * sc2tog; rep from * to last st, sc in last st; join with sl st in first st—7 sts.

Fasten off and sew top of mitten closed using your preferred method of seaming.

Pull all ends to inside and weave in.

Thumbs

With smaller hook and MC, join yarn to first skipped stitch of thumb opening.

Rnd 1: Ch 1, sc in same st as join, FPsc around next st, [sc in next st, FPsc around next st] twice, sc in next st, sc in side of st immediately before thumb ch, sc in next 7 ch, sc in side of st immediately following thumb ch; join with sl st in first st, turn—16 sts.

Rnds 2–9: Ch 1, * sc in next st, FPsc around next st; rep from * around; join with sl st in first st, turn.

Rnd 10: Ch 1, * sc2tog; rep from * around; join with sl st in first st, turn—8 sts.

Rnd 11: Ch 1, * sc2tog; rep from * around, sl st to first st to join—4 sts.

Fasten off and sew top of thumb closed using your preferred method of seaming.

Weave in any rem ends.

Saguaro at Sunset Blanket

Krista Ann

Few things in this world are as breathtaking as a Southwest sunset. Home to over two million saguaros, Saguaro National Park is a spectacular place to take a scenic drive or go for an evening hike. Set up a lawn chair and watch the vibrant colors of the setting sun silhouette these ancient plants across the desert landscape.

Saguaro cacti stand in stark contrast to the setting sun.

DIFFICULTY LEVEL
Intermediate

FINISHED SIZE

Blanket measures 32" (81 cm) wide and 44" (112 cm) tall.

YARN

Worsted Weight (#4 Medium)

Shown in: Berroco Comfort (50% Super Fine Acrylic, 50% Super Fine Nylon); 210 yd [193 m]/3.5 oz [100 g]): #9734 Liquorice (C1), 5 balls, #9732 Primary Yellow (C2), 2 balls, #9743 Goldenrod (C3), 2 balls, #9724 Pumpkin (C4), 1 ball, #9731 Kidz Orange (C5), 2 balls, and #9755 Wild Cherry (C6), 2 balls.

HOOK

Size H/8 (5.00 mm).
Adjust hook size as needed to obtain gauge.

NOTIONS

Scissors; tapestry needle.

GAUGE

22.5 sts × 26 rows = 4" (10 cm) in Single Crochet.

NOTES

If you want to make your blanket larger, you can easily add more rows of black to the bottom and more stitches to the sides of the blanket. You will need more yarn if you choose to make your blanket larger.

This blanket uses intarsia crochet for the color changes.

continued →→

Blanket INSTRUCTIONS

With C1, ch 181 sts.

Row 1: With C1, ch 1, sc in the 2nd ch from hook and in each ch across, turn—180 sts.

Rows 2–17: With C1, ch 1, sc in each st across, turn.

Row 18 (WS): With C1, ch 1, sc in first 38 sts; with C2, sc in next 5 sts; with C1, sc in next 94 sts; with C2, sc in next 5 sts; with C1, sc in next 38 sts, turn—180 sts.

Row 19 (RS): With C1, ch 1, sc in next 12 sts; with C2, sc in next 4 sts; with C1, sc in next 21 sts; with C2, sc in next 7 sts; with C1, sc in next 92 sts; with C2, sc in next 7 sts; with C1, sc in next 37 sts, turn.

Row 20: With C1, ch 1, sc in next 35 sts; with C2, sc in next 12 sts; with C1, sc in next 89 sts; with C2, sc in next 11 sts; with C1, sc in next 15 sts; with C2, sc in next 8 sts; with C1, sc in next 10 sts, turn.

Row 21: With C1, ch 1, sc in next 4 sts; with C2, sc in next 15 sts; with C1, sc in next 12 sts; with C2, sc in next 15 sts; with C1, sc in next 85 sts; with C2, sc in next 15 sts; with C1, sc in next 20 sts; with C2, sc in next 3 sts; with C1, sc in next 11 sts, turn.

C2 will now be the background color.

Row 22: With C2, ch 1, sc in next 2 sts; with C1, sc in next 5 sts; with C2, sc in next 10 sts; with C1, sc in next 15 sts; with C2, sc in next 35 sts; with C1, sc in next 48 sts; with C2, sc in next 2 sts; with C1, sc in next 14 sts; with C2, sc in next 49 sts, turn.

Row 23: With C2, ch 1, sc in next 51 sts; with C1, sc in next 9 sts; with C2, sc in next 5 sts; with C1, sc in next 45 sts; with C2, sc in next 43 sts; with C1, sc in next 5 sts; with C2, sc in next 22 sts, turn.

Row 24: With C2, ch 1, sc in next 76 sts; with C1, sc in next 39 sts; with C2, sc in next 65 sts, turn.

Row 25: With C2, ch 1, sc in next 65 sts; with C1, sc in next 38 sts; with C2, sc in next 77 sts, turn.

Row 26: With C2, ch 1, sc in next 77 sts; with C1, sc in next 38 sts; with C2, sc in next 65 sts, turn.

Rows 27–37: Rep Rows 25 and 26, ending with a Row 25.

Row 38: With C2, ch 1, sc in next 77 sts; with C1, sc in next 37 sts; with C2, sc in next 66 sts, turn.

Row 39: With C2, ch 1, sc in next 66 sts; with C1, sc in next 37 sts; with C2, sc in next 77 sts, turn.

Rows 40–58: Rep Rows 38 and 39, ending with a Row 38.

Row 59: With C2, ch 1, sc in next 67 sts; with C1, sc in next 36 sts; with C2, sc in next 77 sts, turn.

Row 60: With C2, ch 1, sc in next 77 sts; with C1, sc in next 36 sts; with C2, sc in next 67 sts, turn.

Rows 61–71: Rep Rows 59 and 60, ending with a Row 59.

C3 will now be the background color.

Row 72: With C3, ch 1, sc in next 77 sts; with C1, sc in next 36 sts; with C3, sc in next 67 sts, turn.

Row 73: With C3, ch 1, sc in next 67 sts; with C1, sc in next 36 sts; with C3, sc in next 77 sts, turn.

Rows 74–98: Rep Rows 72 and 73, ending with a Row 72.

Row 99: With C3, ch 1, sc in next 66 sts; with C1, sc in next 37 sts; with C3, sc in next 77 sts, turn.

Row 100: With C3, ch 1, sc in next 77 sts; with C1, sc in next 41 sts; with C3, sc in next 62 sts, turn.

Row 101: With C3, ch 1, sc in next 55 sts; with C1, sc in next 48 sts; with C3, sc in next 77 sts, turn.

Row 102: With C3, ch 1, sc in next 77 sts; with C1, sc in next 51 sts; with C3, sc in next 52 sts, turn.

Row 103: With C3, ch 1, sc in next 48 sts; with C1, sc in next 55 sts; with C3, sc in next 77 sts, turn.

Row 104: With C3, ch 1, sc in next 77 sts; with C1, sc in next 58 sts; with C3, sc in next 45 sts, turn.

Row 105: With C3, ch 1, sc in next 43 sts; with C1, sc in next 60 sts; with C3, sc in next 77 sts, turn.

Row 106: With C3, ch 1, sc in next 77 sts; with C1, sc in next 61 sts; with C3, sc in next 42 sts, turn.

Row 107: With C3, ch 1, sc in next 41 sts; with C1, sc in next 62 sts; with C3, sc in next 77 sts, turn.

Row 108: With C3, ch 1, sc in next 77 sts; with C1, sc in next 63 sts; with C3, sc in next 40 sts, turn.

Row 109: With C3, ch 1, sc in next 38 sts; with C1, sc in next 65 sts; with C3, sc in next 77 sts, turn.

Row 110: With C3, ch 1, sc in next 77 sts; with C1, sc in next 67 sts; with C3, sc in next 36 sts, turn.

Row 111: With C3, ch 1, sc in next 35 sts; with C1, sc in next 69 sts; with C3, sc in next 76 sts, turn.

Row 112: With C3, ch 1, sc in next 76 sts; with C1, sc in next 70 sts; with C3, sc in next 34 sts, turn.

Row 113: With C3, ch 1, sc in next 33 sts; with C1, sc in next 71 sts; with C3, sc in next 76 sts, turn.

Row 114: With C3, ch 1, sc in next 76 sts; with C1, sc in next 72 sts; with C3, sc in next 32 sts, turn.

Row 115: With C3, ch 1, sc in next 31 sts; with C1, sc in next 73 sts; with C3, sc in next 76 sts, turn.

Row 116: With C3, ch 1, sc in next 76 sts; with C1, sc in next 74 sts; with C3, sc in next 30 sts, turn.

Row 117: With C3, ch 1, sc in next 30 sts; with C1, sc in next 74 sts; with C3, sc in next 76 sts, turn.

Row 118: With C3, ch 1, sc in next 76 sts; with C1, sc in next 76 sts; with C3, sc in next 28 sts, turn.

Row 119: With C3, ch 1, sc in next 26 sts; with C1, sc in next 78 sts; with C3, sc in next 76 sts, turn.

Row 120: With C3, ch 1, sc in next 76 sts; with C1, sc in next 79 sts; with C3, sc in next 25 sts, turn.

Row 121: With C3, ch 1, sc in next 24 sts; with C1, sc in next 80 sts; with C3, sc in next 76 sts, turn.

Row 122: With C3, ch 1, sc in next 76 sts; with C1, sc in next 80 sts; with C3, sc in next 24 sts, turn.

Row 123: With C3, ch 1, sc in next 23 sts; with C1, sc in next 81 sts; with C3, sc in next 76 sts, turn.

Row 124: With C3, ch 1, sc in next 76 sts; with C1, sc in next 81 sts; with C3, sc in next 23 sts, turn.

continued →→

Row 125: With C3, ch 1, sc in next 22 sts; with C1, sc in next 82 sts; with C3, sc in next 76 sts, turn.

C4 will now be the background color.

Row 126: With C4, ch 1, sc in next 76 sts; with C1, sc in next 82 sts; with C4, sc in next 22 sts, turn.

Row 127: With C4, ch 1, sc in next 22 sts; with C1, sc in next 82 sts; with C4, sc in next 76 sts, turn.

Rows 128 and 129: Rep Rows 126 and 127.

Row 130: With C4, ch 1, sc in next 76 sts; with C1, sc in next 83 sts; with C4, sc in next 21 sts, turn.

Row 131: With C4, ch 1, sc in next 21 sts; with C1, sc in next 83 sts; with C4, sc in next 76 sts, turn.

Rows 132 and 133: Rep Rows 130 and 131.

Row 134: With C4, ch 1, sc in next 76 sts; with C1, sc in next 84 sts; with C4, sc in next 20 sts, turn.

Row 135: With C4, ch 1, sc in next 20 sts; with C1, sc in next 40 sts; with C4, sc in next 8 sts; with C1, sc in next 36 sts; with C4, sc in next 76 sts, turn.

Row 136: With C4, ch 1, sc in next 76 sts; with C1, sc in next 35 sts; with C4, sc in next 11 sts; with C1, sc in next 38 sts; with C4, sc in next 20 sts, turn.

Row 137: With C4, ch 1, sc in next 20 sts; with C1, sc in next 36 sts; with C4, sc in next 13 sts; with C1, sc in next 36 sts; with C4, sc in next 75 sts, turn.

Row 138: With C4, ch 1, sc in next 54 sts; with C1, sc in next 56 sts; with C4, sc in next 14 sts; with C1, sc in next 37 sts; with C4, sc in next 19 sts, turn.

Row 139: With C4, ch 1, sc in next 19 sts; with C1, sc in next 35 sts; with C4, sc in next 16 sts; with C1, sc in next 61 sts; with C4, sc in next 49 sts, turn.

Row 140: With C4, ch 1, sc in next 46 sts; with C1, sc in next 64 sts; with C4, sc in next 17 sts, with C1, sc in next 34 sts; with C4, sc in next 19 sts, turn.

Row 141: With C4, ch 1, sc in next 19 sts; with C1, sc in next 33 sts; with C4, sc in next 18 sts; with C1, sc in next 66 sts; with C4, sc in next 44 sts, turn.

Row 142: With C4, ch 1, sc in next 42 sts; with C1, sc in next 68 sts; with C4, sc in next 18 sts; with C1, sc in next 33 sts; with C4, sc in next 19 sts, turn.

Row 143: With C4, ch 1, sc in next 19 sts; with C1, sc in next 32 sts; with C4, sc in next 19 sts; with C1, sc in next 70 sts; with C4, sc in next 40 sts, turn.

Row 144: With C4, ch 1, sc in next 39 sts; with C1, sc in next 71 sts; with C4, sc in next 19 sts; with C1, sc in next 32 sts; with C4, sc in next 19 sts, turn.

Row 145: With C4, ch 1, sc in next 19 sts; with C1, sc in next 32 sts; with C4, sc in next 19 sts; with C1, sc in next 72 sts; with C4, sc in next 38 sts, turn.

Row 146: With C4, ch 1, sc in next 37 sts; with C1, sc in next 73 sts; with C4, sc in next 19 sts; with C1, sc in next 33 sts; with C4, sc in next 18 sts, turn.

Row 147: With C4, ch 1, sc in next 18 sts; with C1, sc in next 33 sts; with C4, sc in next 19 sts; with C1, sc in next 74 sts; with C4, sc in next 36 sts, turn.

Row 148: With C4, ch 1, sc in next 35 sts; with C1, sc in next 75 sts; with C4, sc in next 20 sts; with C1, sc in next 32 sts; with C4, sc in next 18 sts, ch 1, turn,

Row 149: With C4, ch 1, sc in next 18 sts; with C1, sc in next 32 sts; With C4, sc in next 20 sts; with C1, sc in next 76 sts; with C4, sc in next 34 sts, turn.

Row 150: With C4, ch 1, sc in next 33 sts; with C1, sc in next 77 sts; with C4, sc in next 20 sts; with C1, sc in next 32 sts; with C4, sc in next 18 sts, turn.

Row 151: With C4, ch 1, sc in next 18 sts; with C1, sc in next 32 sts; with C4, sc in next 20 sts; with C1, sc in next 78 sts; with C4, sc in next 32 sts, turn.

Row 152: With C4, ch 1, sc in next 31 sts; with C1, sc in next 79 sts; with C4, sc in next 20 sts; with C1, sc in next 33 sts; with C4, sc in next 17 sts, turn.

Row 153: With C4, ch 1, sc in next 17 sts; with C1, sc in next 33 sts; With C4, sc in next 20 sts; with C1, sc in next 80 sts; with C4, sc in next 30 sts, turn.

Row 154: With C4, ch 1, sc in next 29 sts; with C1, sc in next 81 sts; with C4, sc in next 21 sts; with C1, sc in next 32 sts; with C4, sc in next 17 sts, ch 1, turn,

Row 155: With C4, ch 1, sc in next 17 sts; with C1, sc in next 32 sts; with C4, sc in next 21 sts; with C1, sc in next 82 sts; with C4, sc in next 28 sts, turn.

Row 156: With C4, ch 1, sc in next 28 sts; with C1, sc in next 82 sts; with C4, sc in next 21 sts; with C1, sc in next 32 sts; with C4, sc in next 17 sts, turn.

Row 157: Rep Row 155.

Row 158: With C4, ch 1, sc in next 27 sts; with C1, sc in next 83 sts; with C4, sc in next 21 sts; with C1, sc in next 32 sts; with C4, sc in next 17 sts, turn.

Row 159: With C4, ch 1, sc in next 17 sts; with C1, sc in next 32 sts; with C4, sc in next 21 sts; witch C1, sc in next 83 sts; witch C4, sc in next 27 sts, turn.

Row 160: Rep Row 158.

Row 161: With C4, ch 1, sc in next 17 sts; with C1, sc in next 32 sts; with C4, sc in next 21 sts; witch C1, sc in next 84 sts; witch C4, sc in next 26 sts, turn.

Row 162: With C4, ch 1, sc in next 26 sts; witch C1, sc in next 84 sts; with C4, sc in next 21 sts; witch C1, sc in next 32 sts; with C4, sc in next 17 sts, turn.

Rows 163 and 164: Rep Rows 161 and 162.

Row 165: With C4, ch 1, sc in next 17 sts; with C1, sc in next 32 sts; with C4, sc in next 21 sts; witch C1, sc in next 85 sts; witch C4, sc in next 25 sts, turn.

Row 166: With C4, ch 1, sc in next 25 sts; with C1, sc in next 85 sts; with C4, sc in next 21 sts; witch C1, sc in next 32 sts; with C4, sc in next 17 sts, turn.

Rows 167–169: Rep Rows 165 and 166, ending with a Row 165.

Row 170: With C4, ch 1, sc in next 24 sts; witch C1, sc in next 86 sts; with C4, sc in next 21 sts; witch C1, sc in next 32 sts; with C4, sc in next 17 sts, turn.

Row 171: With C4, ch 1, sc in next 17 sts; with C1, sc in next 32 sts; with C4, sc in next 21 sts; witch C1, sc in next 86 sts; with C4, sc in next 24 sts, turn.

Row 172: With C4, ch 1, sc in next 24 sts; with C1, sc in next 41 sts; with C4, sc in next 6 sts; with C1, sc in next 39 sts; with C4, sc in next 21 sts; with C1, sc in next 32 sts; with C4, sc in next 17 sts, turn.

Row 173: With C4, ch 1, sc in next 16 sts; with C1, sc in next 33 sts; with C4, sc in next 21 sts; with C1, sc in next 38 sts; with C4, sc in next 8 sts; with C1, sc in next 40 sts; with C4, sc in next 24 sts, turn.

Row 174: With C4, ch 1, sc in next 23 sts; with C1, sc in next 40 sts; with C4, sc in next 10 sts; with C1, sc in next 37 sts; with C4, sc in next 22 sts; with C1, sc in next 32 sts; with C4, sc in next 16 sts, turn.

Row 175: With C4, ch 1, sc in next 16 sts; with C1, sc in next 32 sts; with C4, sc in next 22 sts; with C1, sc in next 36 sts; with C4, sc in next 13 sts; with C1, sc in next 38 sts; with C4, sc in next 23 sts, turn.

Row 176: With C4, ch 1, sc in next 23 sts; with C1, sc in next 37 sts; with C4, sc in next 14 sts; with C1, sc in next 36 sts; with C4, sc in next 22 sts; with C1, sc in next 32 sts; with C4, sc in next 16 sts, turn.

Row 177: With C4, ch 1, sc in next 16 sts; with C1, sc in next 32 sts; with C4, sc in next 22 sts; with C1, sc in next 36 sts; with C4, sc in next 15 sts; with C1, sc in next 36 sts; with C4, sc in next 23 sts, turn.

Row 178: With C4, ch 1, sc in next 23 sts; with C1, sc in next 36 sts; with C4, sc in next 15 sts; with C1, sc in next 36 sts; with C4, sc in next 22 sts; with C1, sc in next 32 sts; with C4, sc in next 16 sts, turn.

Row 179: With C4, ch 1, sc in next 16 sts; with C1, sc in next 32 sts; with C4, sc in next 22 sts; with C1, sc in next 36 sts; with C4, sc in next 16 sts; with C1, sc in next 35 sts; with C4, sc in next 23 sts, turn.

C5 will now be the background color.

Row 180: With C5, ch 1, sc in next 23 sts; with C1, sc in next 35 sts; with C5, sc in next 16 sts; with C1, sc in next 36 sts; with C5, sc in next 22 sts; with C1, sc in next 32 sts; with C5, sc in next 16 sts, turn.

Row 181: With C5, ch 1, sc in next 16 sts; with C1, sc in next 31 sts; with C5, sc in next 23 sts; with C1, sc in next 36 sts; with C5, sc in next 17 sts; with C1, sc in next 34 sts; with C5, sc in next 23 sts, turn.

Row 182: With C5, ch 1, sc in next 23 sts; with C1, sc in next 33 sts; with C5, sc in next 18 sts; with C1, sc in next 36 sts; with C5, sc in next 23 sts; with C1, sc in next 31 sts; with C5, sc in next 16 sts, turn.

Row 183: With C5, ch 1, sc in next 16 sts; with C1, sc in next 31 sts; with C5, sc in next 23 sts; with C1, sc in next 36 sts; with C5, sc in next 18 sts; with C1, sc in next 34 sts; with C5, sc in next 22 sts, turn.

continued →→

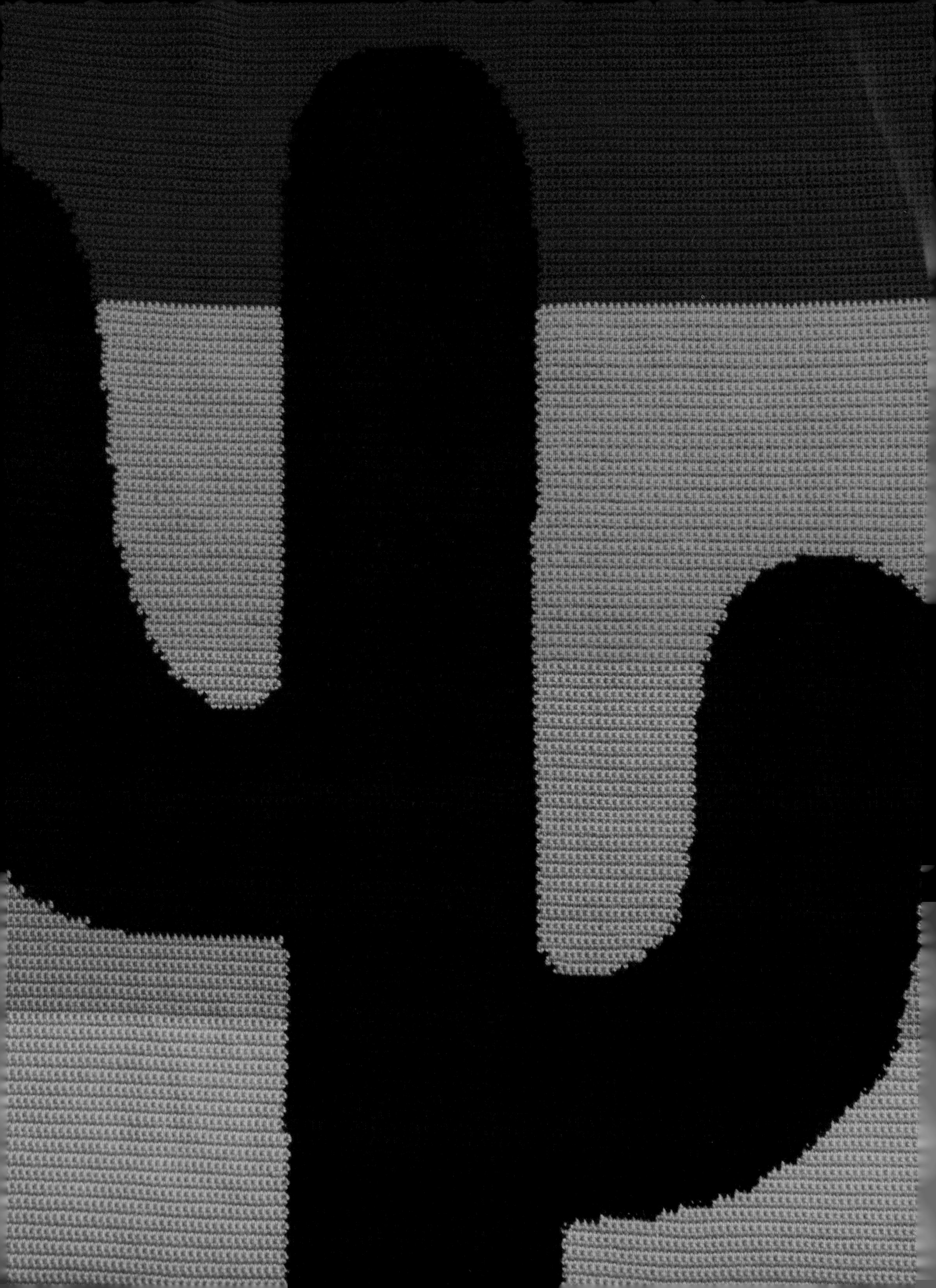

Row 184: With C5, ch 1, sc in next 22 sts; with C1, sc in next 34 sts; with C5, sc in next 18 sts; with C1, sc in next 36 sts; with C5, sc in next 23 sts; with C1, sc in next 31 sts; with C5, sc in next 16 sts, turn.

Row 185: With C5, ch 1, sc in next 16 sts; with C1, sc in next 30 sts; with C5, sc in next 24 sts; with C1, sc in next 36 sts; with C5, sc in next 18 sts; with C1, sc in next 34 sts; with C5, sc in next 22 sts, turn.

Row 186: With C5, ch 1, sc in next 22 sts; with C1, sc in next 33 sts; with C5, sc in next 19 sts; with C1, sc in next 36 sts; with C5, sc in next 24 sts; with C1, sc in next 29 sts; with C5, sc in next 17 sts, turn.

Row 187: With C5, ch 1, sc in next 17 sts; with C1, sc in next 28 sts; with C5, sc in next 25 sts; with C1, sc in next 36 sts; with C5, sc in next 19 sts; with C1, sc in next 33 sts; with C5, sc in next 22 sts, turn.

Row 188: With C5, ch 1, sc in next 22 sts; with C1, sc in next 32 sts; with C5, sc in next 20 sts; with C1, sc in next 36 sts; with C5, sc in next 25 sts; with C1, sc in next 28 sts; with C5, sc in next 17 sts, turn.

Row 189: With C5, ch 1, sc in next 17 sts; with C1, sc in next 28 sts; with C5, sc in next 25 sts; with C1, sc in next 36 sts; with C5, sc in next 20 sts; with C1, sc in next 32 sts; with C5, sc in next 22 sts, turn.

Row 190: With C5, ch 1, sc in next 21 sts; with C1, sc in next 33 sts; with C5, sc in next 20 sts; with C1, sc in next 36 sts; with C5, sc in next 26 sts; with C1, sc in next 26 sts; with C5, sc in next 18 sts, turn.

Row 191: With C5, ch 1, sc in next 19 sts; with C1, sc in next 24 sts; with C5, sc in next 27 sts; with C1, sc in next 36 sts; with C5, sc in next 20 sts; with C1, sc in next 33 sts; with C5, sc in next 21 sts, turn.

Row 192: With C5, ch 1, sc in next 21 sts; with C1, sc in next 33 sts; with C5, sc in next 20 sts; with C1, sc in next 36 sts; with C5, sc in next 28 sts; with C1, sc in next 22 sts; with C5, sc in next 20 sts, turn.

Row 193: With C5, ch 1, sc in next 21 sts; with C1, sc in next 20 sts; with C5, sc in next 29 sts; with C1, sc in next 36 sts; with C5, sc in next 21 sts; with C1, sc in next 32 sts; with C5, sc in next 21 sts, turn.

Row 194: With C5, ch 1, sc in next 20 sts; with C1, sc in next 33 sts; with C5, sc in next 21 sts; with C1, sc in next 36 sts; with C5, sc in next 30 sts; with C1, sc in next 17 sts; with C5, sc in next 23 sts, turn.

Row 195: With C5, ch 1, sc in next 24 sts; with C1, sc in next 14 sts; with C5, sc in next 32 sts; with C1, sc in next 36 sts; with C5, sc in next 21 sts; with C1, sc in next 33 sts; with C5, sc in next 20 sts, turn.

Row 196: With C5, ch 1, sc in next 20 sts; with C1, sc in next 32 sts; with C5, sc in next 22 sts; with C1, sc in next 36 sts; with C5, sc in next 35 sts; with C1, sc in next 7 sts; with C5, sc in next 28 sts, turn.

Row 197: With C5, ch 1, sc in next 70 sts; with C1, sc in next 36 sts; with C5, sc in next 22 sts; with C1, sc in next 32 sts; with C5, sc in next 20 sts, turn.

Row 198: With C5, ch 1, sc in next 20 sts; with C1, sc in next 32 sts; with C5, sc in next 22 sts; with C1, sc in next 36 sts; with C5, sc in next 70 sts, turn.

Rows 199 and 200: Rep Row 197 and 198.

Row 201: With C5, ch 1, sc in next 70 sts; with C1, sc in next 36 sts; with C5, sc in next 22 sts; with C1, sc in next 33 sts; with C5, sc in next 19 sts, turn.

Row 202: With C5, ch 1, sc in next 19 sts; with C1, sc in next 33 sts; with C5, sc in next 22 sts; with C1, sc in next 37 sts; with C5, sc in next 69 sts, turn.

Row 203: With C5, ch 1, sc in next 69 sts; with C1, sc in next 37 sts; with C5, sc in next 22 sts; with C1, sc in next 33 sts; with C5, sc in next 19 sts, turn.

Row 204: With C5, ch 1, sc in next 18 sts; with C1, sc in next 34 sts; with C5, sc in next 22 sts; with C1, sc in next 37 sts; with C5, sc in next 69 sts, turn.

Row 205: With C5, ch 1, sc in next 69 sts; with C1, sc in next 37 sts; with C5, sc in next 22 sts; with C1, sc in next 34 sts; with C5, sc in next 18 sts, turn.

Rows 206 and 207: Rep Rows 204 and 205.

Row 208: With C5, ch 1, sc in next 17 sts; with C1, sc in next 35 sts; with C5, sc in next 22 sts; with C1, sc in next 37 sts; with C5, sc in next 69 sts, turn.

continued →→

Row 209: With C5, ch 1, sc in next 69 sts; with C1, sc in next 37 sts; with C5, sc in next 23 sts; with C1, sc in next 34 sts; with C5, sc in next 17 sts, turn.

Row 210: With C5, ch 1, sc in next 17 sts; with C1, sc in next 34 sts; with C5, sc in next 23 sts; with C1, sc in next 37 sts; with C5, sc in next 69 sts, turn.

Rows 211–215: Rep Row 209 and 210, ending with a Row 209.

Row 216: With C5, ch 1, sc in next 16 sts; with C1, sc in next 35 sts; with C5, sc in next 23 sts; with C1, sc in next 37 sts; with C5, sc in next 69 sts, turn.

Row 217: With C5, ch 1, sc in next 69 sts; with C1, sc in next 37 sts; with C5, sc in next 23 sts; with C1, sc in next 35 sts; with C5, sc in next 16 sts, ch 1, turn

Rows 218 and 219: Rep Rows 216 and 217.

Row 220: With C5, ch 1, sc in next 16 sts; with C1, sc in next 34 sts; with C5, sc in next 24 sts; with C1, sc in next 37 sts; with C5, sc in next 69 sts, turn.

Row 221: With C5, ch 1, sc in next 69 sts; with C1, sc in next 37 sts; with C5, sc in next 24 sts; with C1, sc in next 34 sts; with C5, sc in next 16 sts, turn.

Row 222: With C5, ch 1, sc in next 15 sts; with C1, sc in next 35 sts; with C5, sc in next 24 sts; with C1, sc in next 37 sts; with C5, sc in next 69 sts, turn.

Row 223: With C5, ch 1, sc in next 69 sts; with C1, sc in next 37 sts; with C5, sc in next 24 sts; with C1, sc in next 35 sts; with C5, sc in next 15 sts, turn.

Row 224: Rep Row 222.

Row 225: With C5, ch 1, sc in next 69 sts; with C1, sc in next 37 sts; with C5, sc in next 24 sts; with C1, sc in next 36 sts; with C5, sc in next 14 sts, turn.

Row 226: With C5, ch 1, sc in next 14 sts; with C1, sc in next 36 sts; with C5, sc in next 24 sts; with C1, sc in next 37 sts; with C5, sc in next 69 sts, turn.

Rows 227 and 228: Rep Rows 225 and 226.

Row 229: With C5, ch 1, sc in next 69 sts; with C1, sc in next 37 sts; with C5, sc in next 25 sts; with C1, sc in next 35 sts; with C5, sc in next 14 sts, turn.

Row 230: With C5, ch 1, sc in next 14 sts; with C1, sc in next 35 sts; with C5, sc in next 25 sts; with C1, sc in next 37 sts; with C5, sc in next 69 sts, turn.

Rows 231–233: Rep Rows 229 and 230, ending with a Row 229.

C6 will now be the background color.

Row 234: With C6, ch 1, sc in next 14 sts; with C1, sc in next 34 sts; with C6, sc in next 26 sts; with C1, sc in next 37 sts; with C6, sc in next 69 sts, turn.

Row 235: With C6, ch 1, sc in next 69 sts; with C1, sc in next 37 sts; with C6, sc in next 26 sts; with C1, sc in next 34 sts; with C6, sc in next 14 sts, turn.

Row 236: Rep Row 234.

Row 237: With C6, ch 1, sc in next 69 sts; with C1, sc in next 37 sts; with C6, sc in next 26 sts; with C1, sc in next 33 sts; with C6, sc in next 15 sts, turn.

Row 238: With C6, ch 1, sc in next 15 sts; with C1, sc in next 33 sts; with C6, sc in next 26 sts; with C1, sc in next 37 sts; with C6, sc in next 69 sts, turn.

Row 239: Rep Row 237.

Row 240: With C6, ch 1, sc in next 15 sts; with C1, sc in next 32 sts; with C6, sc in next 27 sts; with C1, sc in next 37 sts; with C6, sc in next 69 sts, turn.

Row 241: With C6, ch 1, sc in next 69 sts; with C1, sc in next 37 sts; with C6, sc in next 27 sts; with C1, sc in next 32 sts; with C6, sc in next 15 sts, turn.

Row 242: With C6, ch 1, sc in next 15 sts; with C1, sc in next 31 sts; with C6, sc in next 28 sts; with C1, sc in next 37 sts; with C6, sc in next 69 sts, turn.

Row 243: With C6, ch 1, sc in next 69 sts; with C1, sc in next 37 sts; with C6, sc in next 28 sts; with C1, sc in next 31 sts; with C6, sc in next 15 sts, turn.

Row 244: With C6, ch 1, sc in next 16 sts; with C1, sc in next 30 sts; with C6, sc in next 28 sts; with C1, sc in next 37 sts; with C6, sc in next 69 sts, turn.

Row 245: With C6, ch 1, sc in next 69 sts; with C1, sc in next 37 sts; with C6, sc in next 29 sts; with C1, sc in next 29 sts; with C6, sc in next 16 sts, turn.

Row 246: With C6, ch 1, sc in next 17 sts; with C1, sc in next 28 sts; with C6, sc in next 29 sts; with C1, sc in next 37 sts; with C6, sc in next 69 sts, turn.

Row 247: With C6, ch 1, sc in next 70 sts; with C1, sc in next 36 sts; with C6, sc in next 29 sts; with C1, sc in next 28 sts; with C6, sc in next 17 sts, turn.

Row 248: With C6, ch 1, sc in next 17 sts; with C1, sc in next 27 sts; with C6, sc in next 30 sts; with C1, sc in next 36 sts; with C6, sc in next 70 sts, turn.

Row 249: With C6, ch 1, sc in next 70 sts; with C1, sc in next 36 sts; with C6, sc in next 31 sts; with C1, sc in next 25 sts; with C6, sc in next 18 sts, turn.

Row 250: With C6, ch 1, sc in next 19 sts; with C1, sc in next 23 sts; with C6, sc in next 32 sts; with C1, sc in next 36 sts; with C6, sc in next 70 sts, turn.

Row 251: With C6, ch 1, sc in next 70 sts; with C1, sc in next 36 sts; with C6, sc in next 32 sts; with C1, sc in next 23 sts; with C6, sc in next 19 sts, turn.

Row 252: With C6, ch 1, sc in next 20 sts; with C1, sc in next 21 sts; with C6, sc in next 33 sts; with C1, sc in next 36 sts; with C6, sc in next 70 sts, turn.

Row 253: With C6, ch 1, sc in next 70 sts; with C1, sc in next 36 sts; with C6, sc in next 35 sts; with C1, sc in next 17 sts; with C6, sc in next 22 sts, turn.

Row 254: With C6, ch 1, sc in next 23 sts; with C1, sc in next 14 sts; with C6, sc in next 36 sts; with C1, sc in next 36 sts; with C6, sc in next 71 sts, turn.

Row 255: With C6, ch 1, sc in next 71 sts; with C1, sc in next 34 sts; with C6, sc in next 39 sts; with C1, sc in next 11 sts; with C6, sc in next 25 sts, turn.

Row 256: With C6, ch 1, sc in next 28 sts; with C1, sc in next 5 sts; with C6, sc in next 42 sts; with C1, sc in next 34 sts; with C6, sc in next 71 sts, turn.

Row 257: With C6, ch 1, sc in next 71 sts; with C1, sc in next 34 sts; with C6, sc in next 75 sts, turn.

Row 258: With C6, ch 1, sc in next 75 sts; with C1, sc in next 34 sts; with C6, sc in next 71 sts, turn.

Row 259: Rep Row 257.

Row 260: With C6, ch 1, sc in next 75 sts; with C1, sc in next 33 sts; with C6, sc in next 72 sts, turn.

Row 261: With C6, ch 1, sc in next 72 sts; with C1, sc in next 33 sts; with C6, sc in next 75 sts, turn.

Row 262–264: Rep Rows 260 and 261, ending with a Row 260.

Row 265: With C6, ch 1, sc in next 73 sts; with C1, sc in next 31 sts; with C6, sc in next 76 sts, turn.

Row 266: With C6, ch 1, sc in next 77 sts; with C1, sc in next 30 sts; with C6, sc in next 73 sts, turn.

Row 267: With C6, ch 1, sc in next 74 sts; with C1, sc in next 29 sts; with C6, sc in next 77 sts, turn.

Row 268: With C6, ch 1, sc in next 78 sts; with C1, sc in next 28 sts; with C6, sc in next 74 sts, turn.

Row 269: With C6, ch 1, sc in next 74 sts; with C1, sc in next 28 sts; with C6, sc in next 78 sts, turn.

Row 270: With C6, ch 1, sc in next 79 sts; with C1, sc in next 26 sts; with C6, sc in next 75 sts, turn.

Row 271: With C6, ch 1, sc in next 76 sts; with C1, sc in next 25 sts; with C6, sc in next 79 sts, turn.

Row 272: With C6, ch 1, sc in next 80 sts; with C1, sc in next 24 sts; with C6, sc in next 76 sts, turn.

Row 273: With C6, ch 1, sc in next 77 sts; with C1, sc in next 22 sts; with C6, sc in next 81 sts, turn.

Row 274: With C6, ch 1, sc in next 82 sts; with C1, sc in next 20 sts; with C6, sc in next 78 sts, turn.

Row 275: With C6, ch 1, sc in next 79 sts; with C1, sc in next 16 sts; with C6, sc in next 85 sts, turn.

Row 276: With C6, ch 1, sc in next 87 sts; with C1, sc in next 12 sts; with C6, sc in next 81 sts, turn.

Rows 277–287: With C6 only, sc in next 180 sts, turn.

Fasten off, weave in all ends. Block blanket lightly, if necessary.

Yellowstone Grand Prismatic Crossbody Bag

Meghan Ballmer

The most iconic hot spring at Yellowstone National Park is the Grand Prismatic Spring. Not only is it the largest hot spring in the United States, but it is also a true wonder of natural beauty, boasting bright blue, green, yellow, and orange hues. Create your own crossbody bag inspired by the stunning beauty of the Grand Prismatic Spring using the unique jasmine stitch and 100 percent cotton yarn.

The colors of the Grand Prismatic Spring are produced by thermopile bacteria living around the edge of the spring.

DIFFICULTY LEVEL

Experienced

FINISHED SIZE

13" (33 cm) height and 14" (35.5 cm) width and 2" (5 cm) depth.

YARN

Worsted Weight (#4 Medium)

Shown in: Universal Yarn Cotton Supreme (100% Cotton; 180 yd [165 m]/3.5 oz [100 g]): #629 Brindle (MC), #638 True Blue (C1), #620 Dutch Blue (C2), #611 Turquoise (C3), #612 Emerald (C4), #630 Sulphur (C5), and #639 Coral (CC6), 1 hank of each.

HOOKS

Size G/6 (4.25 mm) and size H/8 (5.00 mm).

Adjust hook size as needed to obtain gauge.

GAUGE

4 rnds = 5.5" (14 cm) in Jasmine stitch pattern with smaller hook.

NOTIONS

Scissors; tapestry needle; tape measure; two 1" (2.5 cm) D-rings; two 1" (2.5 cm) swivel hooks; one 2" (5 cm) toggle button (optional).

NOTES

Bag is made in four pieces (two Jasmine Stitch circles, one side gusset, and one strap).

Chains at beginning of rnds/rows do not count as a stitch.

STITCH GUIDE

Anchor puff: [Yo, insert hook into indicated sp and draw up a tall lp (about ½" [1.25 cm])] 3 times, yo, draw through all lps on hook while also holding onto the working yarn, insert hook into sp made by working yarn (2 lps on hook), yo and draw through both lps on hook, ch 1 to close puff.

2-puff cluster: [Yo, insert hook into sp at top of last cluster made in this rnd and draw up a tall lp] 3 times (7 lps on hook—horizontal puff made), [yo, insert hook into same sp as last leg of last cluster made in this rnd and draw up a tall lp] 3 times (13 lps on hook), yo and draw through all lps on hook while also holding onto the working yarn, insert hook into sp made by working yarn (2 lps on hook), yo and draw through both lps on hook, ch 1, to close puff.

3-puff cluster: [Yo, insert hook into sp at top of last cluster made in this rnd and draw up a tall lp] 3 times (7 lps on hook—horizontal puff made), [yo, insert hook into same sp as last leg of last cluster made in this rnd and draw up a tall lp] 3 times (13 lps on hook), [yo and insert hook into sp at top of next cluster in prev rnd and draw up a tall lp] 3 times (19 lps on hook), yo and draw through all lps on hook while also holding onto the working yarn, insert hook into sp made by working yarn (2 lps on hook), yo and draw through both lps on hook, ch 1, to close puff.

continued →→

Bag INSTRUCTIONS

Main Circle (Make 2)

Rnd 1: With C1, make a magic ring, work anchor puff in ring, [2-puff cluster] 4 times, 3-puff cluster working last puff into the top of the anchor puff, turn—6 horizontal puffs.

Rnd 2: Work anchor puff into 1st cluster sp (sp at top of last cluster made in prev rnd), *2-puff cluster, 3-puff cluster, rep from * 4 more times, [2-puff cluster] twice, inserting hook into top of anchor puff before finishing last cluster to join, turn—12 horizontal puffs.

Rnd 3: Work an anchor puff into 1st cluster sp, *2-puff cluster, [3-puff cluster] twice, rep from * 4 more times, 2-puff cluster, 3-puff cluster, 2-puff cluster, inserting hook into top of anchor puff before finishing last cluster to join, turn—18 horizontal puffs.

Rnd 4: Work an anchor puff into 1st cluster sp, *2-puff cluster, [3-puff cluster] 3 times, rep from * 4 more times, 2-puff cluster, [3-puff cluster] twice, 2-puff cluster], inserting hook into top of anchor puff before finishing last cluster to join, turn—24 horizontal puffs.

Change to C2.

Rnd 5: Work an anchor puff into 1st cluster sp, *2-puff cluster, [3-puff cluster] 4 times, rep from * 4 more times, 2-puff cluster, [3-puff cluster] 3 times, 2-puff cluster, inserting hook into top of anchor puff before finishing last cluster to join, turn—30 horizontal puffs.

Change to C3.

Rnd 6: Work an anchor puff into 1st cluster sp, *2-puff cluster, [3-puff cluster] 5 times, rep from * 4 more times, 2-puff cluster, [3-puff cluster] 4 times, 2-puff cluster, inserting hook into top of anchor puff before finishing last cluster to join, turn—36 horizontal puffs.

Change to C4.

Rnd 7: Work an anchor puff into 1st cluster sp, [3-puff cluster] 3 times, *2-puff cluster, [3-puff cluster] 6 times, rep from * 4 more times, 2-puff cluster, [3-puff cluster] twice, 2-puff cluster, inserting hook into top of anchor puff before finishing last cluster to join, turn—42 horizontal puffs.

Change to C5.

Rnd 8: Work an anchor puff into 1st cluster sp, [3-puff cluster] 4 times, *2-puff cluster, [3-puff cluster] 7 times, rep from * 4 more times, 2-puff cluster, [3-puff cluster] twice, 2-puff cluster, inserting hook into top of anchor puff before finishing last cluster to join, turn—48 horizontal puffs.

Change to CC6.

Rnd 9: Work an anchor puff into 1st cluster sp, *2-puff cluster, [3-puff cluster] 8 times, rep from * 4 more times, 2-puff cluster, [3-puff cluster] 7 times 2-puff cluster, inserting hook into top of anchor puff before finishing last cluster to join, turn—54 horizontal puffs.

Change to MC.

Rnd 10: *2 sc in next horizontal puff, 3 sc in next horizontal puff; rep from * around, sl st to 1st st to join—135 sts

Fasten off and weave in ends.

Side Gusset

With MC and larger hook, ch 4.

Row 1: Sc in 2nd ch from hook and in each ch across, ch 1, turn—3 sts.

Row 2: Sc in each st across, ch 1, turn.

Row 3: Sc in 1st st, 3 sc in next sts, sc in last st, ch 1, turn—5 sts.

Rows 4–6: Sc in each st across, ch 1, turn.

Row 7: Sc in next 2 sts, 3 sc in next st, sc in next 2 sts, ch 1, turn—7 sts.

Row 8–10: Sc in each st across, ch 1, turn.

Row 11: Sc in next 3 sts, 3 sc in next st, sc in next 3 sts, ch 1, turn—9 sts.

Jasmine Stitch Chart

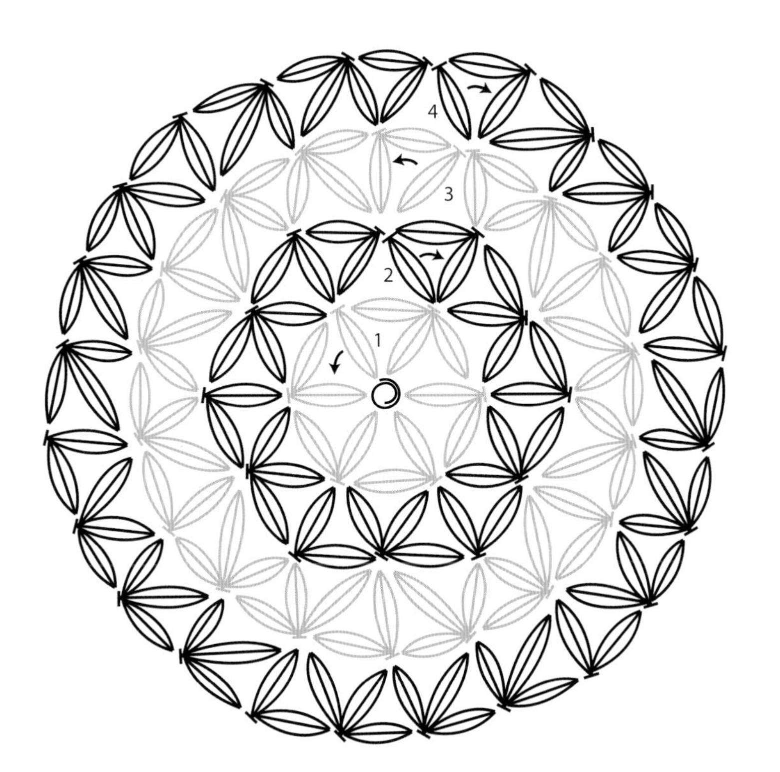

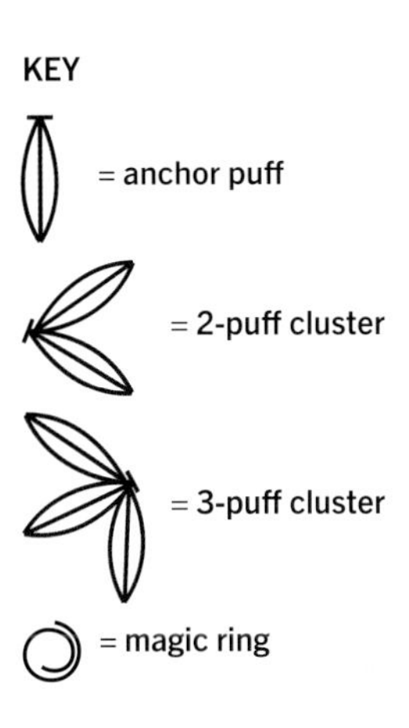

Rows 12–79: Sc in each st across, ch 1, turn.

Row 80: Sc in next 3 sts, sc3tog, sc in next 3 sts, ch 1, turn—7 sts.

Rows 81–83: Sc in each st across, ch 1, turn.

Row 84: Sc in next 2 sts, sc3tog, sc in next 2 sts, ch 1, turn—5 sts.

Rows 85–87: Sc in each st across, ch 1, turn.

Row 88: Sc in next st, sc3tog, sc in next st, ch 1, turn—3 sts.

Row 89–90: Sc in each st across, ch 1, turn.

Fasten off.

Attach Gusset to Circles

Place stitch markers in the first st of Rnd 10 of each circle and in the 46th st from the join. This will mark the opening of the bag.

With the larger hook and MC, attach yarn to the RS of the first circle in the 46th st, ch 1, then insert hook into same st of circle and first row edge of gusset and work an sc. Continue to sc through the next st of the circle and next row edge of the gusset counterclockwise all the way around—90 sc.

Rep this process with the other circle and working into the opposite side of the gusset.

Fasten off and weave in all ends.

continued →→

Strap

With MC and smaller hook, ch 6 leaving a long starting tail.

Row 1: Sc in 2nd ch from hook and each ch across, ch 1, turn—5 sts.

Row 2: Sc in each st across, ch 1, turn.

Repeat Row 2 until strap measures 45" (114 cm).

Fasten off, leaving a long tail for sewing.

Thread the ends of the strap through the bottoms of the swivel hooks. Using the long tails sew the strap to itself about a half inch (1.25 cm) up. Weave in ends to secure.

With a long piece of MC, sew D-rings to either side of gusset about a half inch (1.25 cm) down from the top edge. Weave in ends to secure.

Attach swivel hooks to D-rings.

Button Loop (optional)

With MC and smaller hook, ch 35.

Row 1: Sl st in 2nd back bump from hook and in each back bump across.

Fasten off, leaving a long tail for sewing.

Fold button loop in half and using long tail sew to inside of circle in the 23rd stitch from the side gusset.

On the opposite circle on the RS sew button in place using C1. Center button in the 5th round of the circle.

Weave in any rem ends.

Yosemite Waterfall Scarf

Krista Ann

With more than twenty-five waterfalls inside Yosemite National Park, this California park is a popular place to visit any time of the year. Whether you are taking in the beauty of the 100-foot (30.5-meter) Alder Creek Falls or the impressive 2,425-foot (739-meter) Yosemite Falls, there is no shortage of something spectacular to witness. During the winter months, snow covers the rocky terrain, but water still pours from the falls. Wrap this waterfall-inspired scarf around your neck and soak in all the beauty this national park has to offer.

Nevada Fall seen from the Mist Trail in Yosemite National Park.

DIFFICULTY LEVEL
Intermediate

FINISHED SIZE

Approximately 85" (216 cm) length and 9" (23 cm) width/circumference.

YARN

Bulky Weight (#5, Bulky)

Shown in: Universal Yarn Bamboo Bloom Handpaints (48% Rayon from bamboo, 44% Wool, 8% Acrylic); 154 yd [140 m]/3.5 oz [100 g]): #310 Fuji (MC), 3 skeins.

Rico Design Fashion Light Luxury (71% Alpaca, 22% Wool, 4% Nylon); 142 yd [130 m]/1.76 oz [50 g]): #028 Patina (C1), 1 ball, #012 Ice Blue (C2), 2 balls, #018 Light Blue (C3), 2 balls, and #001 Crème (C4), 1 ball.

HOOKS

Size J/10 (6.00 mm) and size K/10½ (6.50 mm).

Adjust hook size as needed to obtain gauge.

NOTIONS

Scissors; tapestry needle.

GAUGE

14 sts × 16 rows in Single Crochet = 4" (10 cm) with MC and smaller hook.

NOTES

You can make this scarf longer or shorter as desired. If you want to make your scarf longer, you will need more yarn because this pattern uses up nearly all of the MC yarn.

STITCH GUIDE

Loop Stitch: Wrap working yarn around your left index finger forming a lp by taking the yarn over the top of your finger, then down and under the finger and back towards you. Hold finger and lp to back of work. Insert hook in next stitch. Take hook to the right, over the top strand of the lp and grab the bottom strand. Draw the bottom strand through the stitch (2 lps on hook). Take hook to the left, over the top strand of the lp and grab the bottom strand again. Draw the bottom strand through both lps on hook. Drop lp from left index finger—1 Loop stitch made.

continued →→

Scarf INSTRUCTIONS

Beginning of Scarf

With larger hook and 2 strands of C1 held together, ch 25.

Row 1: Loop Stitch in 2nd ch from hook and in each ch across, turn—24 Loop Stitches.

Rows 2–5: Ch 1, Loop Stitch in each st across, turn.

Cut 1 strand of C1 and change to 1 strand each of C1 and C2 held together.

Rows 6–10: Rep Row 2 for 5 rows.

Cut 1 strand of C1 and change to 2 strands of C2 held together.

Rows 11–15: Rep Row 2 for 5 rows.

Cut 1 strand of C2 and change to 1 strand each of C2 and C3 held together.

Rows 16–20: Rep Row 2 for 5 rows.

Cut 1 strand of C2 and change to 2 strands of C3 held together.

Rows 21–25: Rep Row 2 for 5 rows.

Cut 1 strand of C3 and change to 1 strand each of C3 and C4 held together

Rows 26–30: Rep Row 2 for 5 rows.

Cut 1 strand of C3 and change to 2 strands of C4 held together.

Work Row 1 with two strands of C4 a total of 4 times.

Rows 26–30: Rep Row 2 for 5 rows.

Body of Scarf

Cut both stands of C4. Change to 1 strand of MC. Body of Scarf is worked with MC only.

Setup Row: Ch 1, * sc in next 2 sts, 2 sc in next st; rep from * to last 3 sts sc in last 3 sts, turn—31 sts.

Row 1: Ch 1, * sc in next st, hdc in next st, dc in next st, trc in next st, dc in next st, hdc in next st; rep from * to last st, sc in last st, turn.

Row 2: Ch 3, * trc in next st, dc in next st, hdc in next st, sc in next st, hdc in next st, dc in next st; rep from * to last st, trc in last st, turn.

Rep Rows 1 and 2 until scarf measures 74" (188 cm) or 11" (28 cm) short of desired length.

Next row: Ch 1, * sc in next 2 sts, sc2tog; rep from * to last 3 sts, sc in last 3 sts, turn—24 sts.

End of Scarf

Cut MC. Change to larger hook and 2 strands of C4 held together.

Row 1: Ch 1, Loop Stitch in each st across, turn.

Rows 2–5: Ch 1, Loop Stitch in each st across, turn.

Cut 1 strand of C4 and change to 1 strand each of C3 and C4 held together.

Rows 6–10: Rep Row 2 for 5 rows.

Cut 1 strand of C4 and change to 2 strands of C3 held together.

Rows 11–15: Rep Row 2 for 5 rows.

Cut 1 strand of C3 and change to 1 strand each of C2 and C3 held together.

Rows 16–20: Rep Row 2 for 5 rows.

Cut 1 strand of C3 and change to 2 strands of C2 held together.

Rows 21–25: Rep Row 2 for 5 rows.

Cut 1 strand of C2 and change to 1 strand each of C1 and C2 held together

Rows 26–30: Rep Row 2 for 5 rows.

Cut 1 strand of C2 and change to 2 strands of C1 held together.

Work Row 1 with two strands of C4 a total of 4 times.

Rows 26–30: Rep Row 2 for 5 rows.

Cut both strands of C1.

Weave in all tails.

ABBREVIATIONS

beg beginning
BLO back loop only
bp back post
bor beginning of round
C1/2/3/4 contrast color 1/2/3/4
CC contrasting color
ch(s) chain(s)
cm centimeter(s)
dc double crochet
dc5tog double crochet five stitches together
dec('d) decrease(ed)
esc extended single crochet
esc2tog extended single crochet two stitches together
FLO front loop only
FP front post
g gram(s)
hdc half double crochet
hdc2tog half double crochet two stitches together
inc increase
inv invisible
lp(s) loop(s)
m marker; meter(s)
MC main color
mm millimeter(s)
MR magic ring
oz ounce(s)
patt pattern
pm place marker
prev previous
rem remaining
rnd round(s)
RS right side
sc single crochet
sc2tog single crochet two stitches together
sc3tog single crochet three stitches together
sk skip
sl st slip stitch
sp(s) space(s)
st(s) stitch(es)
trc triple crochet
WS wrong side
× times
yd yard(s)
yo yarn over

CROCHET TECHNIQUES

Basic Skills

SLIP KNOT AND CHAIN

All crochet begins with a chain, into which is worked the foundation row for your piece. To make a chain, start with a slip knot. To make a slip knot, make a loop several inches from the end of the yarn, insert the hook through the loop, and catch the tail with the end (1). Draw the yarn through the loop on the hook (2). After the slip knot, start your chain. Wrap the yarn over the hook (yarn over) and catch it with the hook. Draw the yarn through the loop on the hook. You have now made 1 chain. Repeat the process to make a row of chains. When counting chains, do not count the slip knot at the beginning or the loop that is on the hook (3).

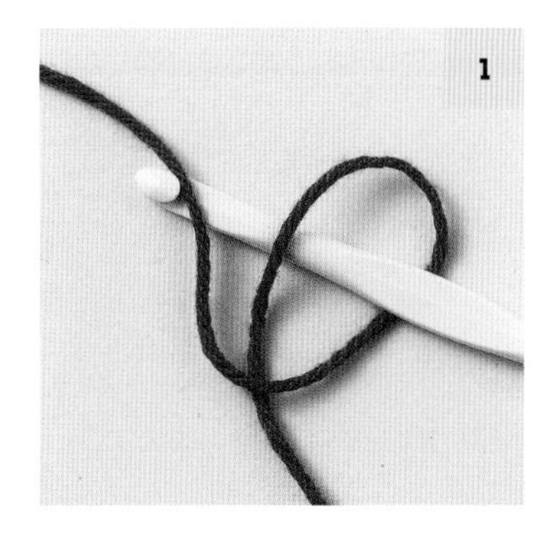
1

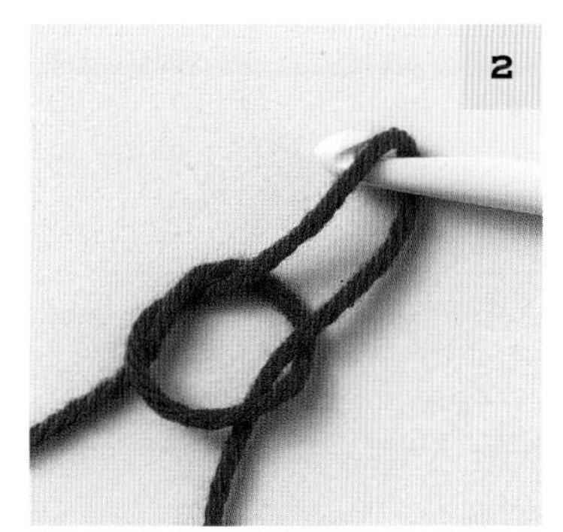
2

3

SLIP STITCH

The slip stitch is a very short stitch, which is mainly used to join 2 pieces of crochet together when working in rounds. To make a slip stitch, insert the hook into the specified stitch, wrap the yarn over the hook (1), and then draw the yarn through the stitch and the loop already on the hook (2).

1

2

SINGLE CROCHET

Insert the hook into the specified stitch, wrap the yarn over the hook, and draw the yarn through the stitch so there are 2 loops on the hook (1). Wrap the yarn over the hook again and draw the yarn through both loops (2). When working in single crochet, always insert the hook through both top loops of the next stitch, unless the directions specify front loop or back loop only.

HALF DOUBLE CROCHET

Wrap the yarn over the hook, insert the hook into the specified stitch, and wrap the yarn over the hook again (1). Draw the yarn through the stitch so there are 3 loops on the hook. Wrap the yarn over the hook and draw it through all 3 loops at once (2).

DOUBLE CROCHET

Wrap the yarn over the hook, insert the hook into the specified stitch, and wrap the yarn over the hook again. Draw the yarn through the stitch so there are 3 loops on the hook (1). Wrap the yarn over the hook again and draw it through 2 of the loops so there are now 2 loops on the hook (2). Wrap the yarn over the hook again and draw it through the last 2 loops (3).

TRIPLE CROCHET

Wrap the yarn over the hook twice, insert the hook into the specified stitch, and wrap the yarn over the hook again. Draw the yarn through the stitch so there are 4 loops on the hook. Wrap the yarn over the hook again and draw it through 2 of the loops so there are now 3 loops on the hook. Wrap the yarn over the hook again and draw it through 2 of the loops so there are now 2 loops on the hook. Wrap the yarn over the hook again and draw it through the last 2 loops.

WORKING THROUGH THE BACK LOOP (BLO)

This creates a distinct ridge on the side facing you. Insert the hook through the back loop only of each stitch, rather than under both loops of the stitch. Complete the stitch as usual.

INCREASING AND DECREASING

To shape your work, you will often increase or decrease stitches as directed by the pattern. To increase in a row or round, you crochet twice into the same stitch, thereby increasing the stitch count by 1. To increase at the end of a row, you chain extra stitches, then turn and work into those stitches, thereby increasing the stitch count.

To decrease in a row or round, you crochet 2 (or more) stitches together as directed, thereby decreasing the stitch count. The technique varies depending on which crochet stitch you are using.

SINGLE CROCHET TWO STITCHES TOGETHER

This decreases the number of stitches in a row or round by 1. Insert the hook into the specified stitch, wrap the yarn over the hook, and draw the yarn through the stitch so there are 2 loops on the hook (1). Insert the hook through the next stitch, wrap the yarn over the hook, and draw the yarn through the stitch so there are 3 loops on the hook (2). Wrap the yarn over the hook again and draw the yarn through all the loops at once.

DOUBLE CROCHET TWO STITCHES TOGETHER

This decreases the number of stitches in a row or round by 1. Wrap the yarn over the hook, insert the hook into the specified stitch, and wrap the yarn over the hook again. Draw the yarn through the stitch so there are 3 loops on the hook. Wrap the yarn over the hook again and draw it through 2 of the loops so there are now 2 loops on the hook. Wrap the yarn over the hook and pick up a loop in the next stitch, so there are now 4 loops on the hook. Wrap the yarn over the hook and draw through 2 loops. Wrap yarn over and draw through 3 loops to complete the stitch.

Advanced Techniques

TWO WAYS TO CROCHET

Working in Rows

Many flat crochet pieces are worked back and forth in rows, beginning with a chain and foundation row. As you crochet, you alternate from right side to wrong side with each row. At the end of each row, you crochet a turning chain of 1 to 4 stitches, depending on the height of the next row of stitches. If the next row will be single crochet, the turning chain is 1 stitch; half-double crochet: 2 stitches; double crochet: 3 stitches; triple crochet: 4 stitches, etc. The directions will tell you how many chains to make. The turning chain counts as a stitch. For instance, the directions may say, "ch 3 (counts as dc)." At the end of each row, the last stitch is worked into the turning chain from the previous row.

Working in Rounds

Another way to crochet is in rounds, going around in continual circles. When working in the round, the right side of the fabric is always facing you. To begin, the directions will tell you to chain a certain number of stitches and join them into a ring by slip stitching into the beginning chain. For the first round, the stitches are worked into the ring (the hook is inserted into the center of the ring), so the stitches will wrap around the beginning chain (1). When you reach your starting point, slip stitch into the beginning stitch. To continue on the next round, the directions will tell you to crochet a starting chain equal to the height of the stitches in the next round. Then continue, crocheting into the stitches of the previous round, and complete the round by stitching into the starting chain (2). When working in rounds, it is necessary to note where the round begins and ends to keep track of rows worked. When working in single crochet, the easiest way to mark your rounds is by inserting a different colored piece of yarn in your work, then carrying it up as you work (3). Using a different colored yarn makes it very easy to see and pulls out easily when your work is done.

If you are working in half double crochet, double crochet, or triple crochet, the chain at the beginning of the row creates a seam stitch, so using a marker is not necessary (4). A typical instruction line might read, "ch 3 to begin the round, * work 1 dc in each of the next 2 sts, 2 dcs in next st (inc made), repeat from * around, join with a Sl st to the top of the beg ch 3." This would complete 1 round. The instructions will vary but they always begin with a starting chain and end with a joining at end of the round.

INVISIBLE JOIN

When working in the round, connecting the end of the round to the beginning can sometimes seem awkward. Here is a way to connect the last stitch in a way that will leave the connection nearly invisible.

End the last stitch but do not join to the beginning with a slip stitch (1). Cut the yarn, leaving a tail several inches long. Pull the yarn through the last stitch and set the hook aside. Thread the tail on a tapestry needle, and run the needle under the beginning stitch, pulling the tail through (2). Insert the needle back through the center of the last stitch of the round and pull the tail to the back of the work (not too tightly) (3). This will join the beginning to the end invisibly (4). Weave the tail into the back of the work.

WHIPSTITCH SEAM

The whipstitch seam works best for sewing straight-edged seams. Holding right sides together, insert needle from front to back through inside loops, bring through and around, and repeat.

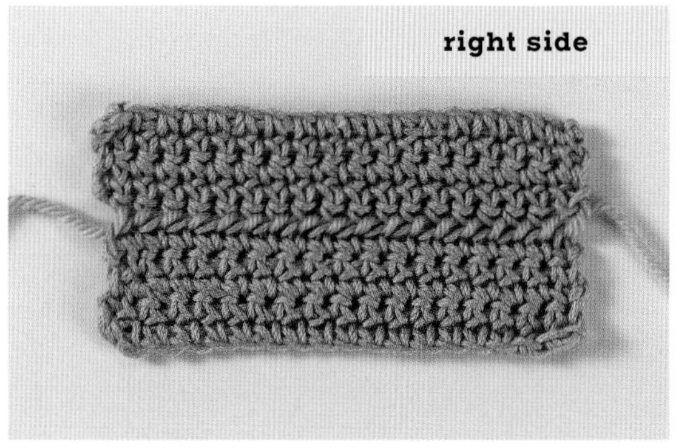

PICKING UP STITCHES FOR BORDERS

You often need to pick up stitches from the edges of a crocheted piece to add a border. Picking up stitches along the sides of a project, the row ends, is the hardest part of giving your crochet pieces a lovely finished look. It is worth the effort to practice this step until you get it right.

The general rule of thumb is to pick up 1 stitch in every other row for single crochet (1). For instance, if you have worked 20 rows of single crochet, you will pick up 10 stitches along the row ends. Pick up 1 stitch for every row for double crochet (2). For instance, if you have worked 20 rows of double crochet, you will pick up 20 stitches. These guidelines work for most people, but not all. Your work must lie flat, and sometimes you will have to experiment to judge how to proceed. If your edges are rippling, like a ruffle, you are picking up too many stitches; if they are pulling in, you are picking up too few stitches.

The best way to get an even edge is to divide the length to be worked into 4 parts. When the first section is done and lies flat, repeat that number of stitches for each of the following 3 sections. Work in every stitch of the top and bottom edges. Always work 3 stitches in each corner to make the project lie flat.

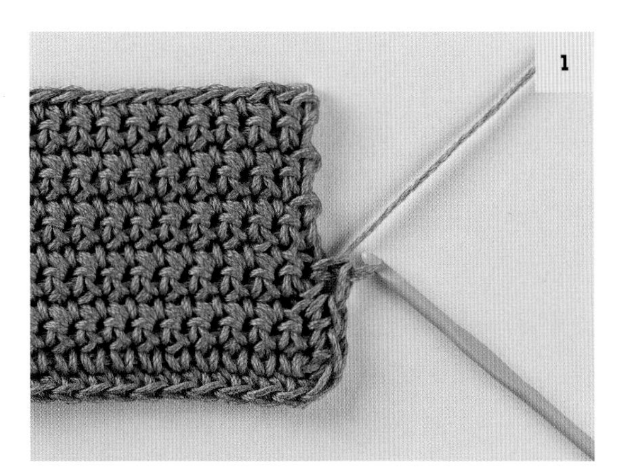

REVERSE SINGLE CROCHET

This stitch is usually used to create a border. At the end of a row, chain 1 but do not turn. Working backward, insert the hook into the previous stitch (1), wrap the yarn over the hook, and draw the yarn through the stitch so there are 2 loops on the hook. Wrap the yarn over the hook again and draw the yarn through both loops. Continue working in the reverse direction (2).

FRONT POST DOUBLE CROCHET

This stitch follows a row of double crochet. Chain 3 to turn. Wrap the yarn over the hook. Working from the front, insert the hook from right to left (left to right for left-handed crocheters) under the post of the first double crochet from the previous row and pick up a loop (shown). Wrap the yarn over the hook and complete the stitch as a double crochet.

BACK POST DOUBLE CROCHET

This stitch follows a row of double crochet. Chain 3 to turn. Wrap the yarn over the hook. Working from the back, insert the hook from right to left (left to right for left-handed crocheters) over the post of the first double crochet from the previous row (shown) and pick up a loop. Wrap the yarn over the hook and complete the stitch as a double crochet.

ABOUT THE CONTRIBUTORS

Rachel Alford

Cozy Nooks Designs
Instagram: @CozyNooksDesigns
Website: cozynooksdesigns.com

Rachel Alford from Cozy Nooks Designs loves taking classic crafts and making them modern and fun. She has a passion for designing both knit and crochet as well as teaching these skills on her YouTube channel, and as a host on the PBS TV show *Knit & Crochet Now!* Always having several WIPs (works in progress) on her hooks/needles while chasing her four kids around, she loves the simple peace that yarn can bring.

Brenda K. B. Anderson

Website: ravelry.com/designers/brenda-k-b-anderson

Brenda K. B. Anderson is a full-time crochet designer and instructor and is also in love with our beautiful national parks. She has visited twenty-eight so far and hopes to someday make it to all of them. Luckily, crochet is completely portable and can be brought along whenever she gets a chance to go camping! Her favorite park is whichever one she is currently visiting (most often Badlands National Park). Her favorite crochet project is the one she is currently working on (most often ridiculously cute amigurumi). Brenda is incredibly proud to be a part of this book!

Meghan Ballmer

Meghan Makes Do
Instagram: @meghanmakesdo
Website: meghanmakesdo.com

Meghan Ballmer is the talented creator behind *Meghan Makes Do*, a beloved blog that focuses on knitting and crochet design. With a passion for fiber arts, Meghan inspires her audience with modern patterns, detailed tutorials, and practical tips. Her approachable style and creative flair make her a go-to resource for both beginners and seasoned crafters looking to expand their skills and create beautiful handmade pieces.

Angel Doherty

Hooked by Angel
Instagram: @HookedbyAngel
Website: hookedbyangel.etsy.com

After her sons left for college, Angel—now an empty nester—discovered a passion for crochet. She specializes in capturing the unique beauty of animals through her intricate creations, ensuring each piece is unique and brimming with personality. No two pieces are identical. Angel has also had the privilege of creating custom designs of cherished pets, which bring immense joy to their owners. She hopes her designs inspire others to create from her patterns and bring as much enjoyment to others as they do to her.

Heather Singell

Storybook Crochet
Instagram: @storybookcrochetco
Website: storybookcrochetco.etsy.com

Heather Singell has been running her crochet design business, Storybook Crochet, for more than seven years and takes joy in creating new crochet patterns to share with others. In addition to her business, she is married to an Army veteran and homeschools her three children. She has been able to travel to many new places, which is something she enjoys doing with her family whenever possible.

RESOURCES

I'd like to extend a special thanks to the yarn companies that provided yarn for the projects in this book. On your next road trip, be sure to stop at the local yarn shop and support these brands or visit their websites to order.

Berroco	berroco.com
Big Twist Value	bigtwistyarn.com
Cascade Yarns	cascadeyarns.com
Dream in Color	dreamincoloryarn.com
Hobby Lobby	hobbylobby.com
Ice Yarns	iceyarns.com
Knitting Fever	knittingfever.com
Knit Picks	knitpicks.com
Lion Brand	lionbrand.com
Premier Yarns	premieryarns.com
Universal Yarn	universalyarn.com
Urth Yarns	urthyarns.com
Yarn Bee	yarn-bee.com
Wool and the Gang	woolandthegang.com

ACKNOWLEDGMENTS

I am constantly reminded how lucky I am to work in an industry that is filled with so many inspiring and talented people. To my editor, Kerry Bogert, thank you for being so much fun to work with and thinking of me for this project. Who would have thought that one phone call all those years ago would have led to years of working together in so many ways! I can't wait to see what kind of stitching magic we create together in the years to come!

Art Director: Heather Godin, Tech Editor: KJ Hay, Project Manager: Liz Weeks, Editorial Director: Joy Aquilino, Cover Illustrator: Alissandra Seelaus, Layout Design: The Sly Studio, and everyone at Quarto Publishing . . . no project this big could ever be accomplished without so many hardworking and talented people. It has been a pleasure working with all of you and I look forward to working together on future projects!

Thank you to Brenda, Heather, Meghan, Rachel, and Angel for contributing to this project. Each one of you was an absolute joy to work with and I am beyond appreciative that you were willing to share your exceptional talents with the world. I could not have asked for a better team of stitchers!

Shout out to the Vanity Knitter's Club in Los Angeles. I miss seeing all of your beautiful faces every week! Even though I'm not there anymore, I'm always with you in yarny spirit!

I am always grateful to the yarn companies and indie dyers that I have the pleasure to work with on projects like this. Your yarns are not just beautiful, but they also spark inspiration in designers like me. Thank you for your generosity and support!

My love for travel, photography, and crafting would not exist without the unconditional love and encouragement from my mom and dad. Thank you for always inspiring me to follow my dreams—no matter how crazy those dreams might be!

And a massive thank you my husband, Garner. You are the love of my life, my best friend, and my favorite travel partner. Words will never express how thankful I am to have you and our fur baby, Phinny, by my side on this crazy adventure we call life.

ABOUT THE AUTHOR

Krista Ann is a nomad who roams the United States with her husband, Garner, and their cat, Dr. Phineas (a.k.a. Phinny), in their 26-foot (8 m) RV travel trailer. On the road since August 2019, they plan to visit as many states and national parks as possible before coming off the road and settling down in a place not yet known.

Knitting since she was 23 and crocheting almost as long, Krista is in her happy place when she has her yarn, hook or needles, Phinny on her lap, and a gorgeous view to enjoy. She finds inspiration in each of the new places they visit. Exploring yarn shops, attending fiber festivals, and meeting new fibery friends along her travels makes the nomadic life all the more interesting.

When Krista isn't on a hike or trying out local pizza shops, she is always doing something creative. She designs knitting and crochet patterns for book projects or yarn companies, including *Knitting Van Gogh* (Weldon Owen, 2024). She sporadically receives calls to work with costume designers to create pieces for the film industry. She has knit or crocheted pieces for major projects including *The Mindy Project*, *Stranger Things*, *Hocus Pocus 2*, *Annabelle Comes Home*, and many more.

Her online knitting app, The Knitting Rockstar Academy, features tours and interviews with yarn shop owners and yarn companies from across the country. In addition, it features behind-the-scenes access into indie dye studios, full project video walkthroughs, and an abbreviation library. There are also endless knitting tips, tricks, and tutorials to up your knitting game.

To learn more about Krista Ann, visit her website at www.explorewithknitsy.com, check out The Knitting Rockstar Academy at www.knittingrockstar.com, or follow her on Instagram @explorewithknitsy.

INDEX

A
abbreviations, 130
Acadia Sunrise Shoulder Bag, 14–17
accessories
- Acadia Sunrise Shoulder Bag, 14–17
- Indiana Dunes Sun Hat, 40–43
- Yellowstone Grand Prismatic Crossbody Bag, 118–123
- Yosemite Waterfall Scarf, 124–127

advanced techniques, 136–139
Alligator Plushie, Everglades, 32–35

B
back past double crochet, 139
Badlands Prairie Dog Plushie, 50–55
bags
- Acadia Sunrise Shoulder Bag, 14–17
- Yellowstone Grand Prismatic Crossbody Bag, 118–123

basic skills, 131–135
Blanket, Saguaro at Sunset, 108–117
borders, 138
Bryce Canyon Hoodoo Socks, 56–60

C
chain, 131
clothing
- Bryce Canyon Hoodoo Socks, 56–60
- Congaree Leg Warmers, 18–21
- Indiana Dunes Sun Hat, 40–43
- Olympic Grand Fir Fingerless Mitts, 86–92
- Petrified Forest Colors Cowl, 94–97
- Rocky Mountains Mittens, 98–106
- Yosemite Waterfall Scarf, 124–127

Coaster Set, Redwood Tree Rings, 98–101
Congaree Leg Warmers, 18–21
Cowl, Petrified Forest Colors, 94–97
Crossbody Bag, Yellowstone Grand Prismatic, 118–123
Cup Cozy, Katmai Grizzly Bear, 80–85

D
decreasing, 134–135
Dish Towel, Great Smoky Mountains Firefly, 36–39
double crochet, 133
double crochet two stitches together, 135
Dry Tortugas Sea Turtle Plant Holder, 22–27

E
easy projects
- Grand Teton Paw Print Picnic Roll, 70–75
- Great Basin Stargazing Pillow, 76–79
- Petrified Forest Colors Cowl, 94–97
- Redwood Tree Rings Coaster Set, 98–101

Everglades Alligator Plushie, 32–35
experienced projects
- Olympic Grand Fir Fingerless Mitts, 86–92
- Yellowstone Grand Prismatic Crossbody Bag, 118–123

F
Fingerless Mitts, Olympic Grand Fir, 86–92
front post double crochet, 139

G
Grand Canyon Wall Hanging, 62–69
Grand Teton Paw Print Picnic Roll, 70–75
Great Basin Stargazing Pillow, 76–79
Great Smoky Mountains Firefly Dish Towel, 36–39

H
half double crochet, 132
home décor
- Dry Tortugas Sea Turtle Plant Holder, 22–27
- Grand Canyon Wall Hanging, 62–69
- Grand Teton Paw Print Picnic Roll, 70–75
- Great Basin Stargazing Pillow, 76–79
- Great Smoky Mountains Firefly Dish Towel, 36–39
- Katmai Grizzly Bear Cup Cozy, 80–85
- Redwood Tree Rings Coaster Set, 98–101
- Saguaro at Sunset Blanket, 108–117
- Shenandoah Gone Hiking Pillow, 44–46

I
increasing, 134–135
Indiana Dunes Sun Hat, 40–43
intermediate projects
- Acadia Sunrise Shoulder Bag, 14–17
- Badlands Prairie Dog Plushie, 50–55
- Bryce Canyon Hoodoo Socks, 56–60
- Congaree Leg Warmers, 18–21
- Dry Tortugas Sea Turtle Plant Holder, 22–27
- Everglades Alligator Plushie, 32–35
- Grand Canyon Wall Hanging, 62–69
- Great Smoky Mountains Firefly Dish Towel, 36–39
- Indiana Dunes Sun Hat, 40–43
- Katmai Grizzly Bear Cup Cozy, 80–85
- Rocky Mountains Mittens, 98–106
- Saguaro at Sunset Blanket, 108–117
- Shenandoah Gone Hiking Pillow, 44–46
- Yosemite Waterfall Scarf, 124–127

invisible join, 137

J
join, invisible, 137

K
Katmai Grizzly Bear Cup Cozy, 80–85

L
Leg Warmers, Congaree, 18–21

M
Mittens, Rocky Mountains, 98–106

N
national parks, map of, 8–9

O
Olympic Grand Fir Fingerless Mitts, 86–92

P
Petrified Forest Colors Cowl, 94–97
picking up stitches for borders, 138
Picnic Roll, Grand Teton Paw Print, 70–75
pillows
- Great Basin Stargazing Pillow, 76–79
- Shenandoah Gone Hiking Pillow, 44–46

Plant Holder, Dry Tortugas Sea Turtle, 22–27
plushies
- Badlands Prairie Dog Plushie, 50–55
- Everglades Alligator Plushie, 32–35

Prairie Dog Plushie, Badlands, 50–55

R
Redwood Tree Rings Coaster Set, 98–101
reverse single crochet, 138
Rocky Mountains Mittens, 98–106
rounds, working in, 136
rows, working in, 136

S
Saguaro at Sunset Blanket, 108–117
Scarf, Yosemite Waterfall, 124–127
Shenandoah Gone Hiking Pillow, 44–46
Shoulder Bag, Acadia Sunrise, 14–17
single crochet, 132
single crochet two stitches together, 135
slip knot, 131
slip stitch, 131
Socks, Bryce Canyon Hoodoo, 56–60
Sun Hat, Indiana Dunes, 40–43

T
techniques, 131–139
traveling, tips for crocheting while, 10
triple crochet, 133

W
Wall Hanging, Grand Canyon, 62–69
whipstitch seam, 137
working through the back loop (blo), 134

Y
Yellowstone Grand Prismatic Crossbody Bag, 118–123
Yosemite Waterfall Scarf, 124–127